S0-ARV-702

# Faith of Our Fathers

Presbyterian & Reformed Life Series

# Faith of Our Fathers

*A Commentary on the Westminster Confession of Faith*

## Wayne R. Spear

Crown & Covenant Publications
Pittsburgh, Pennsylvania

© 2006 by Wayne R. Spear
Published by Crown & Covenant Publications
7408 Penn Avenue
Pittsburgh, PA 15208
www.psalms4u.com

ISBN-10: 1-884527-19-1
ISBN-13: 978-1-884527-19-7

Library of Congress Control Number: 2006901129

First printed in the *Covenanter Witness* of the
Reformed Presbyterian Churches of Ireland and Scotland

All Scripture quotations are taken from the New King James Version,
© Thomas Nelson, Inc.

Page and cover design by Esther Howe. Text and heads are set in
Goudy, Myriad Roman, and Woodtype Ornaments. Cover photo by
John Gratner.

All rights reserved. No part of this book may be reproduced or stored
in a retrieval system in any form by any means (electronic, mechanical, photocopying, recording or otherwise) without the prior written
permission of the publisher.

I lovingly dedicate this book to my dear wife Mary. She has been my faithful helpmate and encourager in all aspects of my life and ministry. Often she has urged me to write, and to have my writing published. In pre-computer days, while caring for our five children, she did the typing for all of my graduate study papers, including the doctoral dissertation. I am glad that, through the kindness of Crown & Covenant Publications, she will see this work in print. "Her worth is far above rubies; the heart of her husband safely trusts her; her children rise up and call her blessed; her husband also, and he praises her" (Prov. 31).

–*Wayne R. Spear*

# Table of Contents

# Preface

The *Westminster Confession of Faith* was composed by the famous Assembly of Puritan ministers and laymen, which met in Westminster Abbey from 1643 to 1648. The Assembly was called together by the Parliament, to give advice about the "further reformation" of the Church of England. The Parliament hoped to bring about agreement among the three kingdoms of the British Isles regarding the doctrine, government, worship, and discipline of the church in those lands.

Those who assembled at Westminster represented the mature fruit of the Protestant Reformation. They consulted the earlier confessional documents of the Reformation, the preaching and writings of Reformed scholars, and, most of all, the Scriptures. They produced a summary of Christian doctrine that it admirable for its comprehensiveness, clarity, practicality, and faithfulness to the Word of God.

In God's providence, the desired agreement among the three kingdoms was not achieved. However, the work of the Westminster Assembly found great acceptance in Scotland. There was a long and severe struggle there with the Stuart kings, who sought to impose their own authority upon the Church of Scotland, culminating in the "Killing Times," when thousands of believers gave up their lives because of their loyalty to Christ and to his truth. After the "Glorious and Bloodless Revolution" of 1688, the Church of Scotland, the Covenanter remnant, and later dissenting churches, all adhered to the *Westminster Confession of Faith* as the statement of their own faith. When immigrants from Scotland and Northern Ireland came to the New World, they brought the *Confession* with them, and it became the official confession of the various Presbyterian churches in America.

Sadly, both in Great Britain and in America, the trend has been away from faithful adherence to the doctrines of the *Confession*. In many Presbyterian churches, the *Confession* is either unknown, or is the object of scorn and criticism. However, there are evidences of a revival of interest in the work of the Westminster Assembly, and in the *Confession* which they produced. There are a growing number of churches in which the *Westminster Confession* is a living document, truly guiding their teaching and preaching (always in subordination to the Scriptures).

One evidence of that renewal of interest is seen in the genesis of this brief commentary on the *Confession*. These chapters were originally written at the request of David McKay, editor of the *Covenanter Witness* of Scotland and Ireland. When that series was completed, Drew and Lynne Gordon, editors of the (American) *Reformed Presbyterian Witness*, asked if the articles might be re-published in that journal. The editors evidently felt that their readers would be interested in, and would be edified by, study of the *Westminster Confession*.

My own interest in the *Confession* began when I read through it during my senior year in high school. My graduate study was concerned with the work of the Westminster Assembly, so that I learned to view the *Confession* within its historical setting. Then, in teaching systematic theology for more than 30 years, I have made use of the *Confession* as a valuable aid to clarity and soundness of doctrine. I am convinced that Christians can profit much from reflection on the *Confession* in the light of the Scriptures.

This work is intended for use by ordinary believers, not by scholars and specialists. It bears the marks of its original publication, with references to the situation in Britain and in America. It should be read with a copy of the *Confession of Faith* at hand, preferably one of the editions that has the Scripture texts written out in full.

I trust that the Lord will use this little work for the building up of His people in their knowledge of the truth, and the application of that truth to their lives.

–*Wayne R. Spear*
*January 2006*

# 1

# Scripture and the Confession

The *Confession*, as a careful summary of the teaching of
Scripture, has been a blessing to Reformed churches
for more than 350 years. It was produced by the careful
work of the great Westminster Assembly, which met during
the English Civil War to advise the Parliament about the
"further reformation" of the Church of England. Commis-
sioners from the Church of Scotland assisted the Assembly,
and it has been in the Reformed Church of Scotland and in
her daughter churches that the *Confession* has had the most
lasting influence.

The members of the Assembly followed the Reformation
principle of *Scripture alone* in writing the *Confession*. That is,
they took the Bible as the ultimate authority for what Christians
are to believe. For that reason, Scripture passages are appended
to every paragraph; indeed, biblical phrases are found frequently
in the wording of the *Confession*. At the same time, they were
not unaware of what believers in earlier generations had discovered in the Bible, so it is clear that earlier confessions and the
works of Christian writers guided the Assembly in its statements

of basic Christian doctrines. The influence of John Calvin, and of British theologians such as William Whitaker and James Ussher, to name a few, is seen in many places in the *Confession*.

Because they were drawing their teaching from the Bible, the Assembly placed a chapter on Scripture at the very beginning of the *Confession*. This was not, as some have charged, because they made the Scripture more important than Christ, but because they were convinced that it is possible to speak the truth about Christ only because we possess in the Bible a trustworthy revelation, which comes from God.

The doctrine of Scripture, explained in the first chapter, includes seven sub-topics: the necessity for the Bible, and the Bible's canon, authority, sufficiency, clarity, languages, and interpretation. We will comment on these sub-topics in order. (The reader should have a copy of the *Confession*, and follow along as the comments are made, taking note of the Scripture passages cited by the *Confession*.) The *Confession*, with the Reformed Presbyterian Testimony alongside, may be downloaded for free from www.reformedpresbyterian.org.

## The Necessity for the Bible

Section one of the chapter tells us why the Scripture is *necessary*. It is necessary, first, because apart from Scripture the people of the world do not know God accurately or savingly. All people have some knowledge of God through "general revelation," God's self-manifestation, which comes through human consciousness ("the light of nature") and by reflection on the reality and the history of the world God has made. Echoing the book of Romans and John Calvin, the *Confession* states that this revelation is insufficient for knowing the way of salvation. In His mercy, God gave another kind of revelation, which does make known the way of life ("*that* his will" refers back to "that knowledge of God and his will which are necessary unto salvation"). This further "special revelation" was then committed *by* God to writing, so that the truth could be preserved from error, and published to the whole world and through all coming ages.

A second reason for the necessity of Scripture is that the *process* of revelation through prophets and apostles came to an end when it reached its climax in Christ. Since then, it is to the Bible that we look if we desire to know God.

## The Canon of the Bible

The question of the *canon* of Scripture is taken up in sections two and three. These sections reflect controversy with the Catholic Church about what particular books make up the written revelation of God. The *Confession* first speaks positively, listing the 66 books that make up the Protestant Bible. In this brief confessional statement, no reasons for listing only these books, are given. We have information, however, on the principles that guided the authors of the *Confession*. Members of the Assembly were familiar with a long discussion and defense of this list published by William Whitaker of Cambridge, in his *Disputation on Holy Scripture*, and undoubtedly agreed with his arguments.

Section three rejects the view of the canon that had been made official in the Catholic Church at the Council of Trent just a century before, which included a number of books found in some copies of the Septuagint. These books, called the Apocrypha, or "hidden" books, the *Confession* regards as merely human writings. Unlike the *inspired* books, they possess no particular authority in the church, and are not included in the rule of faith and life.

It should not be missed that for the Assembly, the doctrine of inspiration was of crucial importance. The Scriptures are not made up of *human* writings, but *divine*. (The *Confession* does not give a separate statement regarding the doctrine of inspiration, or of inerrancy, because those were not disputed points in the 17th century.)

## The Authority of the Bible

The next sections address the topic of the *authority* of the Bible, from two different perspectives. Section four describes the authority that the Scriptures have in and of themselves. This authority, the right to command our belief and action, is not derived from any earthly source. In the matter of the right to rule, the church is not *over* the Bible; rather, the Bible is over the church, which must submit to God's teaching given in Scripture. The Bible has ultimate authority because it comes to us as the Word of God, who is its ultimate Author. Here again is a brief but clear reference to the doctrine of inspiration.

Section five speaks of scriptural authority in another way. How do *we* come to be persuaded of the fact that the Bible is God's true Word, that it possesses authority *over us*? The section mentions three sources of testimony to whom we should listen. The first is the voice of the church. Through all the centuries, there has been a clear consensus in all branches of the Christian Church that the Bible is God's infallible revelation. (Sadly, that consensus has been broken in our century by official actions of some denominations.) That consistent teaching of the church has helped many to believe in the Word of God.

The second testimony to the Word comes from the qualities we find in the Scripture itself: heavenliness of content, the power of its teaching, its majesty of style, its unity, its goal of giving all glory to God, its full revelation of the gospel, and "many other incomparable excellencies." These are not the kind of evidences that would appeal to neutral human reason. They do describe what happens in the *experience* of one who is being drawn by the Holy Spirit to repentance and faith, or who is already a believer. The third kind of testimony is the most important: the inward witness of the Holy Spirit. In regeneration and effectual calling, the Spirit opens our eyes to see the Scripture for what it is and enables us to rest in it as the trustworthy Word of God.

## The Sufficiency of the Bible

The sixth section deals with the sufficiency of the Bible. The Protestant Reformation sought to liberate God's people from the tyranny of the church over their consciences. The

Roman Catholic Church claimed that it was the keeper of unwritten apostolic teaching. Since the traditions were unwritten, the common people had no way of testing the claims of the church. The Confession responds to the Catholic teaching by asserting that "all things necessary for [God's] own glory, man's salvation, faith, and life, is...set down in Scripture: unto which nothing at any time is to be added." Hence, Christians could turn to the Scripture themselves to see whether things taught by the church were true (Acts 17:11). As William Whitaker wrote, "God hath excellently well and wisely provided for his church by delivering to it the scriptures, which contain in themselves a full and perfect body of doctrine sufficient for every man's salvation" (*Disputation*, p. 542).

The *Confession* also warns against "new revelations of the Spirit," because appeal to them implies that God's revelation in Scripture is less than complete. The doctrine of the sufficiency of Scripture is a safeguard against the turmoil and unbiblical teaching of much of what is called the "Third Wave" in Christianity today.

Of course, there are some matters in the life of the church that the Scripture does not address in detail: "circumstances concerning the worship of God, and government of the church, common to human actions and societies." We continue to debate which parts of our church life are "circumstances." In spite of the difficulty in deciding, the distinction between what is circumstantial and what is substantial is an important one. In substantial matters, we must follow the Word. In circumstances, we are free to follow sanctified common sense.

## The Clarity of the Bible

Section seven speaks of the *clarity* of Scripture. The *Confession* rejects the medieval notion that common people cannot understand the Bible, but must depend on the teaching of the church. Instead, all people should study the Bible for themselves, because the things they need to know for salvation are clearly taught there. There are deep and difficult things also, which puzzle the greatest scholars. But, in the beautiful words of John Chrysostom, Scripture is "a river in which a lamb may wade, and an elephant may swim" (Whitaker, p. 400).

## The Languages of the Bible

The *languages* of the Bible is the subject of section eight. In controversies between the Catholic Church and the Protestants, the former insisted that the Latin Vulgate was the authoritative translation. With the rediscovery of the Hebrew and Greek manuscripts, the followers of the Reformation believed that they had more accurate copies of the Bible than the Vulgate, which contained many errors in translation. The *Confession* goes on to express concern for the common people, who cannot read the Bible in the original languages. So that they may have the great blessing of reading and studying the Word of God for themselves, the Scriptures are to be translated into the languages of the people. The vision of John Wycliffe and William Tyndale, earlier translators of the Bible into English, is here embraced and passed on to succeeding generations.

## The Interpretation of the Bible

The last two sections deal with the *interpretation* of Scripture. Rejecting the fanciful method of interpretation which found multiple, artificial meanings in the words of the Bible, the *Confession* declares that we must look for the simple, clear meaning of each passage. To do that, Scripture must be compared with Scripture. We can understand the more difficult passages in the light of the clearer passages, and we gain insight into the meaning of biblical words by seeing how they are used in many places in the Bible. When disagreements arise in the understanding of Scripture, the *Confession* declares that the final authority is not to be found in the church, but in continuing, patient, prayerful study of the Scriptures. When God's people do not agree, they are to keep praying and studying until the Holy Spirit brings them to a unity of belief. In this way, Word and Spirit can, over time, bring God's people to a common belief about what Scripture teaches. This is the basis for a true ecumenicity in the Church, rather than compromise and negotiations resembling those used to bring about mergers between corporations.

B. B. Warfield wrote of this chapter, "There is certainly in the whole mass of confessional literature no more nobly conceived or ably wrought-out statement of doctrine than the chapter, 'Of the Holy Scriptures' which the Westminster Divines placed at the head of their *Confession* and laid at the foundation of their system of doctrine. It has commanded the hearty admiration of all competent readers" (*The Westminster Assembly and its Work*, p. 155). The more we reflect on the chapter, the more inclined we are to agree with Warfield's assessment. It directs us to the way of life pointed out by both Moses and Jesus: "Man shall not live by bread alone, but by every word that proceeds from the mouth of God" (Deut. 8:3; Matt. 4:4). ⊕

# 2

# Of God and the Holy Trinity

The *Confession* begins with a description of the *source* of the content of Christian belief. The revealing activity of God, and particularly the Scripture, is given to us so that we might know the way of salvation and how we may enjoy fellowship with God now and in the life to come. Then, because "the fear of the Lord is the beginning of wisdom" (Prov. 1:7), the *Confession* immediately deals with the nature of the God who reveals Himself in Scripture.

In its doctrine of God, the *Westminster Confession of Faith* is not seeking to break new ground. Some of its wording is drawn directly from the Bible: "living and true God" is from 1 Thessalonians 1:9; "working all things according to the counsel of his own…will" is from Ephesians 1:11. We hear a clear echo of Exodus 34:6-7 in the first paragraph: God is "longsuffering, abundant in goodness and truth, forgiving in iniquity, transgression, and sin…and who will by no means clear the guilty." The writers of these words are not indulging in rational speculation about God; they are responding in faith to His testimony to Himself in Scripture. We must do the same.

The words of this chapter also reflect earlier creeds of the Christian Church. "Without body, parts, or passions" is found in the *Thirty-Nine Articles of the Church of England* (article I, par. 8), and also in James Ussher's *Irish Articles of Religion* (1615). The third section parallels the view of the Trinity expressed in the so-called Athanasian Creed, which was used in the Western Church since the 9th century. Like the Puritans, we should see ourselves as belonging to the true church of God that has been preserved through all of history. We share in the historic Christian faith, whose basic beliefs are embodied in the *Westminster Confession.*

The structure of this chapter is not easy to discern. In general, we may say that the first section speaks of *God as He is in Himself*: the second, with *God in relation to His creation*, and the third, clearly, with *God as Trinity*. We must limit our discussion in this brief study to a few particular points. For further study, one should reflect carefully on the Bible proof texts, which are given, and read a good commentary on the *Confession*, such as recent ones by G. I. Williamson or Rowland Ward.

## God as He Is in Himself

Section 1 stresses the infinity and perfection of God, by using superlatives in speaking of His various characteristics. He is "a most pure spirit...most wise, most holy, most free, most absolute...most loving...most just." We may know of these qualities in the created world in a limited way, but God is greater than anything we know. We must be careful not to bring Him down to our level.

One of the ways God differs from us is in His absolute spirituality. As a spirit (John 4:24), He is not subject to any of the limitations that are inherent in matter. The Bible speaks of God's hands, ears, and eyes, but such statements are to be taken as word pictures, pointing to God's actions in the world, His perfect knowledge, and His responsiveness to our prayers.

The statement that God is "without passions" may raise some questions. In its description of God, the *Confession* speaks of him as "loving" and as "hating all sin." Are these also metaphorical expressions? We must surely remove from our concept of God all that is impure and inappropriate in our own emotions. But it would rob many statements of Scripture of their meaning if we were to say that there is nothing like emotion in God. "Just as a father has compassion on his children, so the Lord has compassion on those who fear him" (Ps. 103:13). Our own experience of a father's love is used in Scripture to teach us about God's love for us.

In the present theological climate, something should be said about the incomprehensibility of God. This chapter is filled with statements of what we know of God, because the truth has been made available to us in the Bible. There have been many modern theologians, like Soren Kierkegaard and Karl Barth, who have rejected the possibility of our having any real knowledge of the one who they describe as "Wholly Other." God is so different from us, they say, that He remains hidden from us even in His revelation to us. In contrast, however, Jesus spoke of our possessing eternal life through *knowing* the living and true God (John 17:3). God is so great that we who are creatures can never know Him fully and completely; but we can know Him truly on the basis of His Word.

## God in Relation to His Creation

The second section of the chapter emphasizes the self-sufficiency or independence of God from His creation. God relates to us, He deals lovingly and graciously with us, but He does not *need* us. The *Confession* here is faithfully repeating the message of Paul the Apostle to the philosophers in Athens (Acts 17:24-25). In our existence, and in our redemption, God takes the initiative, and we are utterly dependent upon Him. He owes us nothing, but has the right to do with us as He pleases. He is sovereign.

The section speaks also of the unlimited knowledge of God. In His knowledge also, God is independent of us. His knowledge is not contingent—that is, it is not dependent on factors outside of Himself. Reality is what it is, the future will be what it will be, because God has decreed it. His plan is the foundation of His knowledge. As will be said in a later chapter, election of persons to salvation is not based on God's prior knowledge of their independent action, but is unconditional.

This view of God and His dealings with us is very humbling, but it is true, because it is what is taught in the Word. It is not a bad thing that we are totally dependent on God, while He is independent of us, because "he is most holy in all his counsels, in all his works, and in all his commands." He has the absolute right to require of us worship, service, and obedience. If the church is to have vibrant spirituality and meaningful worship, this view of God as sovereign and holy must be at the heart of her faith. "Be still, and know that I am God" (Ps. 46:10).

## God as Trinity

The final section of the chapter sets forth in simple terms the doctrine of the Trinity.

A full understanding of the Trinity is beyond our grasp, but its basic elements can be stated fairly simply: (1.) There is only one God. (2.) The Father is God, and the Son is God, and the Holy Spirit is God. (3.) Father, Son, and Holy Spirit are distinct persons.

The oneness of God is stated earlier in this chapter, supported by appropriate texts of Scripture. That the Father is God is accepted by all who claim to be Christian. The deity of Christ is presented in Chapter 8 of the *Confession*. Curiously, the *Confession* has no separate discussion of the full deity of the Holy Spirit; later Presbyterians have either added a chapter on the Holy Spirit to the *Confession*, or have included the doctrine of the Holy Spirit in a separate Testimony.

The distinction of persons has been helpfully explained by Lorraine Boettner: "Thus we see that the Persons within the Godhead are so distinct that each can address the others, each can love the others, the Father sends the Son, the Father and Son send the Spirit, the Son prays to the Father, and we can pray to each of them. They act and are acted upon as subject and object, and each has a particular work to perform. We say that they are distinct persons, for a person is one who can say 'I,' can be addressed as 'thou,' and who can act and be the object of action" (*Studies in Theology*, p. 91). The final sentence of the section expresses the truth that the personal distinctions among Father, Son, and Spirit are eternal.

The *Westminster Confession* is sometimes criticized for the order in which it discusses the various subjects taught in the Scripture. It is suggested that it would have been better to *begin* with Christ and the gospel. However, we should view this chapter on the nature of God as a preparation for the presentation of the gospel, which comes later in the *Confession*.

We must know something of who God is before we can understand the necessity and the possibility of having a relationship with Him. We must know that He hates sin before we can appreciate our need for a Savior. And we must be persuaded that He is "most loving, gracious, merciful, long-suffering, abundant in goodness and truth, forgiving iniquity, transgression, and sin," before we will come to Him in faith so that we may receive His great gift of salvation in Christ.

It might be possible to deal with the contents of this chapter in an impersonal, merely intellectual way, but to do so would mean missing a great blessing. J. I. Packer tells us what we need to do: "How can we turn our knowledge *about* God into knowledge *of* God? The rule for doing this is demanding, but simple. It is that we turn each truth that we learn *about* God into matter for meditation *before* God, leading to prayer and praise *to* God….And it is as we enter more and more deeply into this experience of being humbled and exalted that our knowledge of God increases, and with it our peace, our strength, and our joy. God help us, then, to put our knowledge about God to this use, that we all may in truth 'know God' " (*Knowing God*, pp. 18-19).     ⊕

# 3

# The High Mystery
# of Predestination

We begin our reflection on this chapter at the chapter's end: "So shall this doctrine afford matter of praise, reverence, and admiration of God, and of humility, diligence, and abundant consolation, to all that sincerely obey the Gospel." If we rightly understand what is taught here of God's plan, or the doctrine of predestination, our response will be deeply experiential: praise for God, and comfort for ourselves.

Although the *Confession* deals with predestination earlier than John Calvin does in the order of teaching, its purpose is the same: to connect our assurance of salvation with God's unshakable plan (see Calvin's *Institutes*, Book III, Chap. 21). This is in keeping with what we find in Romans 8, where groaning believers, conscious of their own weakness, are comforted by being reminded that what God has purposed to do, namely to bring them to glory, He will surely accomplish.

## God's Plan for Creation

The chapter begins with two sections that speak of God's decree, or plan, as it applies to the whole of created reality.

"Whatever comes to pass" in the created world happens because God ordained, or determined before time began, that it would happen. Romans 11:36, the doxology which concludes Paul's longest discussion of predestination teaches this: "For from Him and through Him and to Him are all things. To Him be the glory forever! Amen" (see also Eph. 1:11).

To guard against misunderstanding, several points are carefully stated. God's plan covers everything, including sin, but we must not think that God sins, or that He simply causes sin to happen. The Bible clearly teaches both the sovereignty of God and human responsibility, but we cannot fully understand how they are related. This is why the *Confession* speaks of the "high mystery of predestination," which must be handled with care.

Further, the operation of God's plan does not violate "the will of the creatures." Calvinists believe in the freedom of the will, when those words are rightly understood (see Chap. 9)! As responsible human beings, we make real choices. Those choices are expressions of our natures, of our hearts. Sinful people will freely choose to do what is evil. The teaching of the Bible is that even in choosing to do evil, in a mysterious way sinners are carrying out God's purposes. The outstanding example of this is Judas' betrayal of Christ (see Acts 2:23).

A third point is stated in difficult language: "Nor is the liberty or contingency of second causes taken away." This simply means that God's plan is not carried out by magic, but that cause and effect are built into the creation. God fulfills His plan by ordaining all the causes or means by which His goals will be accomplished. We live in an orderly universe because it is governed by God's plan. Scientists who deny the reality of God would have no work to do if it were not for the dependability of the "second causes" established by God's decree.

Sections 2 and 5 make the point that God's decree or plan is *unconditional*; that is, it is not based on foreknowledge. Romans 8:29, which mentions foreknowledge before predestination, is speaking of "knowledge" in the sense of an intimate, personal relationship, which was planned before-hand. It would give the true meaning if we were to translate the verse, "those on whom he set his love beforehand, he also did predestinate." That which is future does not yet exist, except in the mind of God. God knows what will happen in the future because He has planned the future.

## God's Plan for Human Beings and Angels

The focus of the chapter narrows in the remaining sections, to speak of God's plan as it applies to one aspect of the creation, namely the eternal destination of angels and of human beings. "Some angels and men are predestinated unto everlasting life, and others fore-ordained to everlasting death." The emphasis, understandably, is on the salvation (and condemnation) of sinful humans.

It is this teaching of the *Confession* (and of the Scripture) that is most offensive to unbelievers, and even to many Christians who are unwilling to accept the clear teaching of the Bible on this point. (For an exposition of the biblical teaching, the reader is urged to ponder the scriptures given in the footnotes of the *Confession*, and to study a book like Boettner's *The Reformed Doctrine of Predestination*.) If we accept the Bible as our ultimate rule for faith and life, then we must humble ourselves under its teaching about predestination even if, at the beginning, it goes against what we would like to believe.

The *purpose* of God's plan is "for the manifestation of his glory." In those whom He chooses for salvation, God demonstrates the riches of His grace. In those whom He passes by, He shows His power and justice. As we try to make sense out of the world and our experiences in it, it is necessary for us to realize that there is a greater purpose than our own happiness or comfort. God is making Himself known in creation, providence, history, and redemption. At the climax of history, an innumerable company will proclaim, "To Him who sits on the throne, and to the Lamb, be blessing and honor and glory and dominion forever and ever" (Rev. 5:13).

Like God Himself, His plan is *eternal* and *unchangeable*. While He interacts with us, and responds to our needs and prayers, He does not change. What He has purposed, He will do. Proud King Nebuchadnezzar was forced to acknowledge that "He does according to His will in the host of heaven and among the inhabitants of earth, and no one can ward off His hand or say to Him, 'What hast Thou done?' " (Dan. 4:35).

God's plan includes not only the final outcome of things, but also the intermediate steps by which the outcome will be brought to pass. A famous American jurist who was hostile to biblical Christianity once uttered some harsh words that have become a common saying in our culture: "damned if you do and damned if you don't."

He meant that, according to Calvinism, if one were not one of the elect, he would be condemned even if he believed in Christ and asked forgiveness for his sins. People often say that if the doctrine of predestination is true, then it is unnecessary for us to pray, to evangelize, or to do anything else. Such views fail to understand that God uses our decisions and actions to carry out His plan. "For we are His workmanship, created in Christ Jesus for good works, which God prepared beforehand, so that we would walk in them" (Eph. 2:10).

Those whom God has chosen for salvation do not fly immediately to heaven. They are led there step by step. God brings them into contact with His people; they hear the gospel; the Holy Spirit renews their hearts; they repent and believe. They are not only justified, but are sanctified, so that their lives give evidence that God's Spirit is at work in them. They keep on trusting and striving for holiness throughout life. God's gracious plan for them includes not only the destination, but also the journey.

This chapter expresses the doctrine some call "double predestination," because it states that God not only chose some to be saved, but that He determined to "pass by" others, and "to ordain them to dishonor and wrath for their sin." This is a hard teaching, but it must be said that "single predestination" is not a possibility. If God chose some, but not all, to be saved, then He necessarily did not choose others. It is true that the Bible emphasizes election more than it does the "passing by," but it clearly teaches both. If this is difficult to accept, then we must humbly accept God's right to do according to His own holy will with sinful men and women. "Who are you, O man, who answers back to God?...Does not the potter have a right over the clay, to make from the same lump one vessel for honorable use and another for common use?" (Rom. 9:20-21).

Chapter 18 of the *Westminster Confession* deals with the assurance of salvation. It is also mentioned here, when Section 8 says that those who listen obediently to God's Word "may, from the certainty of their effectual vocation, be assured of their eternal election." This means that as we find in our own experience that the Holy Spirit has made us able to understand the gospel, to be aware of our sinfulness and condemnation, and has persuaded us to trust in Christ alone for our salvation, we have evidence that God from all eternity has chosen us to be His children, to receive His forgiveness, and to enjoy fellowship with Him forever.

Understood in this way, the doctrine of predestination gives us reason to praise God, to be humble and diligent in our life before Him, and to have confidence that there is absolutely nothing which can separate us from Christ's love.　⊕

# 4

# Evolution and the Confession

In our time, the doctrine of creation receives a great deal of attention from the media and in the culture in general. In the United States, this is because of legal controversies over the teaching of evolution and/or creation in tax-supported schools. Those who believe what the Bible teaches on this point are generally regarded as behind the times, uninformed, or ignorant. Some Christians are therefore tempted to surrender to the general culture with regard to their understanding of beginnings, although they still cling to the Christian and biblical view of human destiny and salvation through Christ.

## Understanding God Through Creation

Such a surrender, however, has grave consequences for the Christian faith as a whole. The doctrine of creation is not an isolated and unimportant matter, but is foundational to our understanding of God, of the world of reality, and of the meaning and purpose of human existence.

In Chapter 2 of the *Westminster Confession*, God is distinguished from all other aspects of reality in that He is eternal and self-sufficient, i.e., not dependent on anything or anyone else. In Chapter 4, that biblical understanding of God is brought to bear on the question of origins. God is eternal; all other things have a beginning. God is independent; all other things, including human beings, exist only because it pleased (and pleases) God to call them into being. (When the *Confession* says that it "pleased" God to create, it means that it was not *necessary* for Him to do so.) God is the ultimate goal of creation: all things are made to display His glory. Creatures are not an end in themselves; they manifest the glory of the One who made them.

The absence of a true doctrine of creation, then, will have a harmful effect on our view of God. If God did not create all things, then something else would be eternal, something else would be independent, some other entity or power would demand our ultimate devotion and service. We would wickedly "worship and serve the creature rather than the Creator, who is blessed for ever. Amen!" (Rom. 1:25).

Departure from the worship of the Creator is precisely what we observe in our culture. It denies creation and attributes the existence, complexity, order, and beauty of the world to (in the words of Francis Shaeffer) "the impersonal, plus time, plus chance." Those who hold an evolutionary view of origins cannot study nature for long before they are filled with a sense of wonder. They begin to speak of how "Evolution" or "Nature" or even "Mother Nature" has designed a certain organ or organism to perform in a marvelous way.

## Understanding Human Origins

Denial of creation is particularly damaging in relation to human existence and meaning. The second section of this chapter gives attention to the Bible's teaching about human origins. Human sexuality, and differences of gender, are part of God's good creation. Human beings differ from other earthly creatures in their capacity for thought and reflection and in the fact that they will not pass out of existence at death. (Contrary to Greek thought, our souls are not *inherently* immortal; both our souls and our resurrected bodies will exist eternally because God wills it to be so.)

Humans are made after the image of God. That is, we have minds and consciences, and we are made in such a way that we may reflect in the world the character of our Maker. In Adam and Eve before they sinned, and in those who become new creatures in Christ, there is not only the potential for this, but the actuality. Like God, His redeemed people are righteous and holy, not perfectly, of course, but really. Like God, they speak the truth, are generous to those in need, speak in a way that builds people up, are kind, tenderhearted, forgiving, and pure (Eph. 4:20–5:4).

Humans have the power of choice. Before the Fall, they were free to choose good or evil. Since the Fall, we choose according to our sinful nature. In Christ, we are again given the power to choose good. As moral beings, we have an inescapable sense of right and wrong ("the law written on the heart"). We were created to have blessed fellowship with God, and given a position of stewardship and responsibility over the rest of creation.

In our unbelieving culture, this biblical view of human origin, dignity, and destiny is largely rejected. The famous behavioral psychologist, B. F. Skinner, wrote a book called *Beyond Freedom and Dignity* in which he sets forth the view that human beings, as the products of an impersonal and unthinking process of evolution, are completely determined in their behavior by their heredity and their environment. There is, in his view, no "freedom" for humans to make choices, and no "dignity" derived from being created in the image of God. A man is an organism that responds to stimuli in his environment, and no more. "To man as man we readily say good riddance" (pp. 200-201).

Bertrand Russell, the British philosopher, wrote in *Mysticism and Logic* that from now on, human understanding must be built on a foundation of unyielding despair. "Brief and powerless is Man's life; on him and all his race the slow doom falls pitiless and dark. Blind to good and evil, reckless of destruction, omnipotent matter rolls on its relentless way; for Man, condemned today to lose his dearest, tomorrow himself to pass through the gate of darkness, it remains only to cherish, ere yet the blow falls, the lofty thoughts that ennoble his little day" (pp. 56-57).

Such views, it is claimed, are based on a scientific understanding of reality, and must therefore be accepted by all intelligent people. However, Christians must not surrender to unyielding despair. We need not and we must not accept such a view of the world simply because it claims to be scientific.

## The Falsity of Evolution

Despite all the propaganda about evolution, it is increasingly clear that it does not rest on a solid foundation of scientific investigation. When Darwin first propounded his theory in 1859, he acknowledged that empirical evidence for it, whether from the study of fossils, or from direct observation, was very weak. He hoped that continuing research would supply the evidence that was then absent.

Recently, two significant books have been published that contend that Darwin's hope has not been fulfilled: Michael Denton's *Evolution: A Theory in Crisis*, and Phillip Johnson's *Darwin on Trial*. Both authors make the case that, after more than a century of intensive effort, convincing fossil evidence of transitional forms is still missing, and discoveries in genetics and molecular biology have made Darwinian evolution even more difficult to accept.

Citing evolutionist Richard Dawkins, Phillip Johnson calls Darwinism "the blind watchmaker thesis" because, according to the theory, natural selection operates blindly, without plan or purpose, and yet its results have the *appearance* of design, "as if by a master watchmaker." On the basis of the astounding lack of evidence which he has described, Johnson then states the following conclusion: "Darwinian evolution with its blind watchmaker thesis makes me think of a great battleship on the ocean of reality. Its sides are heavily armored with philosophical barriers to criticism, and its decks are stacked with big rhetorical guns ready to intimidate any would-be attackers....But the ship has sprung a metaphysical leak, and the more perceptive of the ship's officers have begun to sense that all the ship's firepower cannot save it if the leak is not plugged. There will be heroic efforts to save the ship...but in the end reality will win" (pp. 169-170).

The *Westminster Confession of Faith* was written in a "pre-scientific" age, but its teaching about the origin of the universe and of the human race is not out of date, because it is founded on the Word of God, which "abides for ever" (1 Pet. 1:25). An evolutionary worldview lacks a truly scientific basis, and leads to despair. A worldview based on the Bible's teaching about creation leads to hope, and life with meaning and responsibility. Believers in Christ must continue to hold to the doctrine of creation, and thus to speak a message of hope and meaning in a despairing world.　　　　⊕

# 5

# What Providence Is—and Is Not

The fifth chapter of the *Westminster Confession of Faith*, "Of Providence," follows naturally the discussion of creation from Chapter 4. The world is neither eternal nor self-created, but exists because of the sovereign act of the infinite, eternal, and unchangeable Creator. Once created, the world does not continue by its own power, but remains totally dependent on the same Creator, both for its existence and its direction.

## Providence and Dependence on God

The *Confession* cites Paul's address to the philosophers at Athens in Acts 17: "He gives to all life, breath, and all things....in Him we live and move and have our being" (vv. 25-28). Before speaking of Christ and the resurrection, Paul gave the outlines of the Christian worldview: God is the Creator of all things, and it is by His power that the world remains in existence. As our culture moves away from its Christian heritage, increasingly we will need to do the same thing: to seek to have people understand that they are dependent on God for their very existence, and that this gives God a claim on their lives.

Historically, God's work of providence has been discussed under the headings of preservation and government. *Preservation* refers to God's continuing activity in maintaining the existence and order of the creation. *Government* means that God is directing the operations of the universe and the events of human history to accomplish His purposes. The *Confession* speaks of preservation in using of the word "uphold." Government is expressed by the words, "direct, dispose, and govern."

The providence of God extends to every aspect of the world, "from the greatest even to the least." Providentially, kingdoms rise and fall, and not even a sparrow falls to the ground without the Father's will. In the small and great things that affect our lives, it is a great comfort to know that the world is not running out of control, but that it is being directed to fulfill the great and good purposes of God!

## Providence and Human Decision

In the view of the Bible and of the *Confession*, providence is the accomplishment in time of the eternal plan of God. In our limited human understanding, this presents some problems. An earlier Reformed *Confession*, the *Second Helvetic Confession*, stated it like this: "We disapprove of the rash statements of those who say that, if all things are managed by the providence of God, then our efforts and endeavors are in vain" (Chap. VI). In its answer, that *Confession* refers to Paul's experience in his voyage to Rome.

In a storm, Paul was given assurance that he would be brought safely to Rome. Yet, when some of the sailors prepared to abandon ship, Paul said, "unless these men stay in the ship, you cannot be saved" (Acts 27:31). God's plan would be carried out through the skilled efforts of the sailors, that is, by the use of means.

The *Westminster Confession* addresses the same question in a different way, in the second section of chapter 5:

"Although, in relation to the foreknowledge and decree of God, the first Cause, all things come to pass immutably, and infallibly: yet, by the same providence, He ordereth them to fall out, according to the nature of second causes, either necessarily, freely, or contingently."

Critics of the *Westminster Confession* often say that it is too "scholastic"—overly academic and philosophical. That criticism is unjustified, as a careful study of the *Confession* will show. In this section, however, there is an example of scholasticism. In speaking of first and second causes, and using the concepts of necessity, contingency, and freedom, the *Confession* echoes the language of Thomas Aquinas, who in turn was making use of the concepts of Aristotle. Ordinary people find this language very difficult. (Indeed, none of the commentaries on the *Confession* consulted for this article attempted to explain these words.)

From Aquinas' discussion, "second causes" refers to the means God uses in His providential rule, like preserving our lives by providing us with food. Second causes that operate "necessarily," refer to what some call laws of nature—the orderly processes which are constant, like the rising of the sun or the boiling of water at a certain temperature. Causes that operate "freely" or "contingently" are those in which there is variability. The foremost example would be the unforced decisions of human beings.

The *Confession* is affirming (unlike modern behaviorists like B. F. Skinner) that we freely make real decisions, and that those decisions have significance in the course of history. Yet these decisions are used by God to carry out His plans. Joseph's brothers decided freely to sell him into slavery. Though that decision was evil, Joseph declared that "God meant it for good" (Gen. 50:20). The death of Jesus on the cross came about through the wicked decisions of Judas and others, yet Peter said at Pentecost that it came about by the "determined counsel and foreknowledge of God" (Acts 2:23).

Ordinarily, we are told in the third section, God makes use of means in His providential activity. However, He is not limited to this way of working, but "is free to work without, above, and against them." Here the *Confession* introduces the subject of the miraculous. We must avoid two errors in thinking about miracles. One is the mistake of the modernists and materialists, who regard nature as a closed system in which God cannot or does not act. The other error is to think that God intervenes occasionally in the world to work a miracle, but otherwise lets the world operate on its own. It is better to distinguish between the ordinary and the extraordinary operations of providence. God is always and everywhere active in His world. There are "laws of nature" only because of the regularity which characterizes God's ordinary providence. Miracles are rare, precisely because they are extraordinary and therefore unpredictable. Whether God heals indirectly, by the use of medical treatment, or directly, as in the biblical miracles, the glory is His, because He did it.

## Providence and Evil

The fourth section of the chapter deals with the vexing questions of the relation of the providence of God to the presence of evil in His world. The "problem of evil" continues to be a matter for philosophers to discuss, but it also touches all of us as we try to make sense of the troubling experiences that come to us. Simply stated, the problem is this: "If God is in control of all things, and if He is perfectly good, how can evil exist?"

The most obvious possible answers are that (1) God is not in control; (2) He is not good; or (3) Evil does not exist. In America, a popular book by Rabbi Kushner, *When Bad Things Happen to Good People* has given the first answer: Bad things happen because God cannot prevent them. It is small comfort to be told that we have a well-meaning but helpless God when we face tragedy!

The *Confession* does not attempt to give a simplistic answer to the problem of evil. It gives us the biblical perspective, which is all we need in order to live. The Fall of Adam, and other sins of men and angels, are permitted by

God, in such a way that He is not "the author or approver of sin." But more than mere permission is involved: God limits sin. We may think here of the experience of Job. Satan was permitted to bring severe suffering upon him, but only as far as God allowed; his life had to be spared. Further, God orders and governs evil, so that it accomplishes God's purposes. We must be content to humble ourselves under the mighty hand of God when we suffer or see others suffering, knowing that He does all things well, and that "all things work together for good to those who love God, to those who are the called according to His purpose" (Rom. 8:28).

Sections five and six of the chapter draw a contrast between God's providential dealings with His own children, and with the wicked and ungodly. In section five we see the deep, experiential, and pastoral focus of the *Confession* (decidedly not scholastic!).

One purpose in the sufferings of God's own people is chastisement. Such sufferings are intended to show us our sin and weakness, to humble us, to enhance our reliance on the Lord, and to make us more watchful. Instead of the perennial question "Why?" when we are going through hard times, we should ask "What for?—what good purpose is God working out in my life through this suffering?"

Section six gives a sobering but biblical statement of the providence of God in the lives of the wicked. We daily observe what is described here: "They harden themselves, even under those means which God useth for the softening of others." But we do not know the details of God's counsel; and we should pray and labor that some, whose hearts now appear to be hardened, may be softened by the grace of God.

The chapter closes with a word of comfort for God's people. His providence in "a most special manner" takes care of His Church. The church is often despised, often persecuted, often appears to be weak and struggling. But we have the promise of Christ, "I will build my church" (Matt. 16:18). The central purpose in the providence of God is to glorify His own name by the full and final redemption of His people. As we reflect on God's providence, we may sing, from Psalm 102,

> The LORD in glory has appeared,
> Has built up Zion strong and fair,
> And He the destitute has heard,
> Has not despised their humble prayer.

# 6

# The Fall, Sin, and Punishment

These days, in America at least, there is much public conversation about sin. Political scandals, "ethnic cleansing" in various countries, and terrorism within our own shores have led many people to wonder aloud about the reasons for such terrible actions. There is often a sense of amazement; because in modern culture there is a deep conviction that human nature is basically good. It has been more difficult in the light of recent events to reconcile that belief in fundamental human goodness with our experience.

The *Westminster Confession of Faith*, following the Scripture, gives an account of human nature that is much more realistic than that of unbelieving culture. Dreadful acts of violence and immorality are only the most extreme examples of a pervasive reality: Men and women are not "basically good." Jesus taught that a tree bears fruit according to its nature; evil thoughts, words, and deeds come from a fallen, sinful nature.

## The Origin of Evil

The *Confession* traces human sinfulness back to Adam

and Eve: "Our first parents, being seduced...by Satan, sinned in eating the forbidden fruit." After the creation of the first humans, God looked upon everything He had made, and declared it to be "very good" (Gen. 1:31). Sin was not a part of God's original creation; it entered the human race through a historical event that took place in space and time. This is an important point because to treat the events of the early chapters of Genesis as mythical leads to the conclusion that sin is an inevitable element of the human condition. If that were so, there would be no possibility of our being delivered from it. The biblical hope, by contrast, is that one day believers in Christ will be made "perfectly holy and happy" (see 1 John 3:1–2).

Many thinkers have pondered the mystery involved in the origin of evil. The *Confession* is content to echo what was said in the previous chapter about evil and the providence of God. Evil is included in God's "wise and holy counsel," but by way of permission, and under His control. We should follow the godly restraint of the *Confession* in such deep matters.

Efforts to explain fully the origin of evil almost always lead to denial of some aspect of the truth revealed in Scripture. "The secret things belong to the Lord our God, but the things revealed belong to us and to our sons forever, that we may observe all the words of this law" (Deut. 29:29).

## The Consequences of Sin

The second section of this chapter of the *Confession* describes the consequences of sin for Adam and Eve. No longer do they reflect, as the image of God, His qualities of knowledge, righteousness, and holiness (see Eph. 4:24; Col. 2:10). No longer do they enjoy the intimate fellowship with God that had been their privilege. They have become dead to the things of God, and the process of physical death, or mortality, is already at work in them. They are defiled in all aspects of their being.

These dreadful consequences were not limited to Adam and Eve; they are passed down to all of their descendants (except Jesus).

## Guilt and Corruption

Section 3 describes what theologians call "original sin." There are two aspects of original sin: guilt and corruption.

We are connected with Adam in such a way that the guilt of his first sin is imputed to us. This is the teaching of Romans 5:12-19, where Paul makes an extended comparison of Adam and Christ. The heart of the comparison is this: "So then as through one transgression there resulted condemnation to all men [i.e., to all who are descended from Adam, except Jesus], even so through one act of righteousness there resulted justification of life to all men [i.e., to all who are united to Christ by faith]" (Rom. 5:18). Our justification is through imputation, as God reckons Christ's obedience and suffering to our account. So it is with our condemnation: it begins with the imputation of Adam's transgression to our account. This is a hard teaching to accept, but we must bow before the Scripture, and be humble enough to believe God's Word. We should remember that the first sin involved substituting merely human wisdom for what God had clearly spoken (Gen. 3:1-5).

In this chapter, the *Confession* does not describe the exact nature of our connection with Adam. The next chapter, on God's covenant with man, will state that the connection is covenantal.

The other aspect of original sin is our "corrupted nature," which we inherit from our parents, going back through the generations to Adam and Eve. Before we trusted in Christ, we lived "in the lusts of our flesh, indulging in the desires of the flesh and of the mind, and were by nature children of wrath" (Eph. 2:3). Human beings are capable of terrible acts of wickedness because they are not basically good, but sinful by nature. The amazing thing is not that people do evil things, but that there is any good behavior at all from those whose nature is described in such passages as Romans 1:18-32 and 3:10-23.

On the basis of such passages, the *Confession* speaks in the fourth section of our total depravity. We are "utterly indisposed, disabled, and made opposite to all good, and wholly inclined to all evil." This bleak picture of human nature is given not to drive us to utter despair, but to drive us to Christ. It is foundational to a Calvinistic understanding of salvation. We are saved by the gracious and powerful work of God, because we cannot save ourselves, cannot even make the first move toward God, unless He works in us to give us a new nature (John 3:3-7).

## Sin in the Life of the Believer

In later chapters of the *Confession*, the gospel of salvation will be fully described. Anticipating that later discussion, this chapter goes on to speak of sin in the life of the believer. Section 5 makes the point that though our sinful nature is pardoned and mortified (put to death) in Christ, it is still present with us as long as we are in this life.

In many places the Scripture describes the struggle in the life of the Christian against sin. We are assured of ultimate victory, but in the meantime we must resist the devil, pray to escape temptation, put off the old nature with its deeds, etc. "If we say that we have no sin, we are deceiving ourselves, and the truth is not in us" (1 John 1:8).

That statement rejects "perfectionism"—the teaching that it is possible in this life to be free from all known sin. Scripture forbids us to claim such perfection. However, Reformed believers sometimes are tempted to despair of ever making significant progress in holiness. Sometimes our opposition to perfectionism leads to a perverse pride in our imperfection! When this is the case, we need to refresh our confidence in the doctrine of sanctification, and remember what the Scripture says: "His divine power has granted to us everything pertaining to life and godliness,…He has granted to us His precious and magnificent promises, so that by them you might become partakers of the divine nature, having escaped the corruption that is in the world by lust" (2 Pet. 1:3-4). We are not promised perfection, but we are promised abundant grace, which will enable us to make real progress in holiness.

The chapter closes on a gloomy note. It tells us what our sin results in: guilt, God's wrath, death, misery. Some churches seek consciously to avoid such themes, feeling that they will drive people away. However, before we can appreciate the good news of the gospel, we have to hear the bad news of our sin and guilt, our fearful danger of being exposed to the righteous wrath and judgment of God. Said Jesus, "I did not come to call the righteous, but sinners, to repentance" (Matt. 9:13).

# 7

# The Confession of
# Covenant Theology

This chapter contains an aspect of the *Westminster Confession* that distinguishes it from all the Reformed Confessions which preceded it. The *Confession* embodies the "covenant theology" that was developed in Scotland and Switzerland in the latter part of the 16th century.

The term "covenant" appears very frequently in the Bible (almost 300 times in the KJV), and an understanding of the significance of the covenant concept is essential to a proper understanding of the message of salvation.

The covenant concept points, in its central meaning, to relationship. The terms of a covenant specify the basis, nature, and conditions of a relationship. This is so whether it be a covenant between equals, such as marriage, or international treaties (Mal. 2:14; Gen 21:22-32), or a covenant in which God enters into a relationship with His creatures.

## How God Covenants with His People

When God enters into a covenant with us humans, He sovereignly determines the terms of the covenant, setting forth its promises, commands, and penalties. We are called upon to respond to God's declaration of the covenant by embracing the promises in faith, and by purposing to obey the commands, which He gives. This pattern of covenant response is seen in the *Confession*'s definition of saving faith: "By this faith, a Christian believeth to be true whatsoever is revealed in the Word, for the authority of God Himself speaking therein; and acteth differently upon that which each particular passage thereof containeth; yielding obedience to the commands, trembling at the threatenings, and embracing the promises of God for this life, and that which is to come" (14:2).

In the covenant theology of the *Westminster Confession*, two covenants are described: the Covenant of Works, and the Covenant of Grace. (In some explanations of covenant theology, there is a third, inter-trinitarian covenant, called the Covenant of Redemption, which underlies the Covenant of Grace.) Broadly speaking, the Covenant of Works may be thought of as setting forth the law of God, and the Covenant of Grace as the proclamation of the gospel.

These two terms, the "Covenant of Works" and the "Covenant of Grace," do not appear in precisely these words in Scripture. Like the word "Trinity," they are theological terms that accurately express what the Scripture teaches.

## The Covenant of Works

The Covenant of Works expresses the terms upon which God established a relationship with Adam immediately after his creation. The parties of the covenant were God and Adam. The latter, however, did not act for himself alone, but by God's appointment was the covenant head, or representative, of the human race. The command of the covenant was "perfect and perpetual obedience" to the revealed will of God. In Genesis 2, the revealed will of God included a specific "thou shalt not": the prohibition of eating the fruit of the tree of the knowledge of good and evil. In addition, Adam also had the divine directions for his life recorded in the first chapter of Genesis: the "creation ordinances" of marriage, stewardship over the rest of creation, and the Sabbath. We infer that Adam had an intuitive, divinely implanted knowledge of the law of God. The apostle Paul tells us that, even after the Fall, the Gentiles, who do not possess the written law, have the work of the law written on their hearts (Rom. 2:14-15). If they know something of God's law, how much more must Adam have known God's will, since he was created after the image of God, in knowledge, righteousness, and holiness (see 4:2).

The penalty of the covenant is plain: "In the day you eat thereof, you will surely die" (Gen. 2:17). This was the dread consequence of disobedience: the end of intimate fellowship with God, and ultimately the separation of the soul from the body in physical death and everlasting destruction from the presence of the Lord (2 Thess. 1:9). The promise of the covenant is inferred from the penalty. If disobedience would bring death, then obedience would result in continued, blessed fellowship with God, which is the essence of life (John 17:3).

Although this arrangement with Adam and his posterity is not called a covenant in Genesis, it has all the elements of a covenant: parties, commands, penalty, promise. In Hosea 6:7, Adam's transgression is referred to as the breaking of a covenant. The parallel that is drawn between Adam and Christ in Romans 5:12-21 also indicates that a covenant is involved, because our relationship with Christ is clearly covenantal.

This covenant is called a Covenant of Works because of its stress on obedience. In the *Westminster Shorter Catechism* (Q. 12), more happily, it is called the Covenant of Life because of its gracious promise. And there was grace in the Covenant of Works. The *Confession* indicates that any beneficial relationship between a creature and the Creator involves condescension on His part. He was under no obligation to offer the blessing of life in His presence to the human race, but it pleased Him to do so out of His kindness.

If we understand that God deals with mankind in terms of the Covenant of Works, some puzzling passages in the New Testament become clearer. For example, when the rich young ruler came to Jesus asking what he must do to have eternal life, why did Jesus respond by directing him to the Ten Commandments (Luke 18:18-23)? The answer is that, before he could know his real need for the grace of Christ, he had to see himself as a covenant-breaker who had failed to keep God's commands, and who therefore deserved the penalty of death under the Covenant of Works. Or consider the otherwise strange section in Paul's presentation of the gospel in Romans. In Romans 2:5-11, Paul seems to be preaching salvation by works: "God will give to each person according to what he has done. To those who by persistence in doing good seek glory, honor, and immortality, he will give eternal life. But for those who are self-seeking and who reject the truth and follow evil, there will be wrath and anger." What Paul is doing is applying the convicting power of the Covenant of Works, because we must know that we are under its penalty before we will be ready to throw ourselves upon the mercy of God in Christ Jesus.

## The Covenant of Grace

To say "the Covenant of Grace" is another way of saying "the gospel." According to the *Confession*, in this covenant God "freely offereth unto sinners life and salvation by Jesus Christ, requiring of them faith in Him that they may be saved" (7:3). The gospel offer, the proclamation of the terms of the Covenant of Grace, goes out to all lost sinners. We are commanded to go into all the world and preach the gospel to every creature (Mark 16:15).

In one sense, then, the Covenant of Grace may be said to be conditional. Its command is to believe, and the promised salvation is given only to those who believe. However, sinners by themselves are hostile to God and the gospel, and will not come to Christ for life (John 5:40; 6:44). Therefore, those whom God has chosen from eternity are enabled to fulfill the condition of the Covenant of Grace. God promises "to give unto all those that are ordained unto life His Holy Spirit, to make them willing and able to believe" (7:3).

Covenant theology emphasizes the unity of Scripture, and of the plan of salvation. It stands in opposition to modern dispensationalism, which insists that there is a fundamental difference between God's dealings with Israel, on the one hand, and the Church, on the other. This chapter, in sections 5 and 6, describes some of the differences between the Old and New Testaments, but insists that "There are not therefore two covenants of grace, differing in substance, but one and the same, under various dispensations."

Evidence for the unity of the plan of salvation may be seen in the prominence in Scripture of the covenant made with Abraham (Gen. 12:1-3; 15:1-6; 17:1-12; 18:16-19). The deliverance of the children of Israel from Egypt was in fulfillment of God's covenant promise to Abraham (Ex. 3:1-10). Paul teaches that everyone who believes in Christ is a child of Abraham, and is justified by faith, just as Abraham was (Rom. 4; Gal. 3). When the company of the redeemed is portrayed in Revelation 7:9 as an innumerable multitude from every nation, we see the fulfillment of the promise made to Abraham, that his descendants would be as the stars of heaven and the sand of the sea in number, and that in him all the nations of the world would be blessed.

At the heart of the covenant theme in Scripture, occurring literally from Genesis to Revelation, are these words from God: "I will be your God, and you shall be my people."

What a privilege it is to know that we are the people of God, to whom He has bound Himself by covenant! Therefore, in all the trials and uncertainties of life, we live with the assurance that He will never leave us or forsake us, but will be our God to all eternity (Heb. 13:5-6; Ps. 48:14). ⊕

# 8

# The Heart of the Gospel

If any chapter of the *Westminster Confession* can be said to contain the heart of the Christian gospel, it is this one. In eight brief sections it summarizes what the Scriptures teach about the person and work of the Lord Jesus Christ. A person who understands this chapter will possess the knowledge that is necessary for salvation (2 Tim. 3:15). A Christian who desires to win others to Christ will profit much from a careful study of this chapter, and of the Scripture passages given in support of it.

## God's Eternal Purpose

The first section traces Christ's saving work back to the eternal purpose of God. The Son of God, the second person of the Godhead, was chosen and ordained to be the Mediator between a holy God and sinful men and women. Thus Christ does His saving work in fulfillment of an arrangement or agreement made among the Persons of the Trinity before the world began.

Some theologians call this the Covenant of Redemption. We find the same perspective in Ephesians 1: 3-14 and 1 Peter 1:1-5.

## The Identity of the Savior

The second section tells us clearly the identity of the Savior. He is truly and eternally God. In the incarnation, He became truly and permanently man. He is one person, the God-man, the Messiah.

In these few words, the *Confession* takes up and passes on to us the results of centuries of discussion and controversy about the person of Christ in the early Church. For God to become man was an event that is absolutely without parallel in the history of the creation. So it took the Church a long time to come to an accurate understanding of the Bible's teaching about the identity of Jesus. In the Council of Nicea in 325 A.D., and in the Council of Chalcedon in 451 A.D., the Church expressed the consensus that had been reached.

The language of this section of the *Confession* echoes that of Nicea and Chalcedon. The first sentence is from Nicea, especially the assertion that Christ is "of one substance [essence, reality] with the Father." The second sentence is from Chalcedon, which emphasized that there are two natures in Christ, the divine and the human, and yet only one person. The third sentence gives a summary: "Which person is very [truly] God, and very man, yet one Christ, the only Mediator between God and man."

We are to believe these things about Christ, not just because the early church councils declared them, but because they are taught in the Bible. Therefore, as in all study of the *Confession*, the Scripture texts listed need to be studied carefully.

## Christ's Qualifications

The third section describes the qualifications of Christ to be the Messiah, the Savior of sinners. It does so by drawing together in a kind of collage many biblical expressions about Him. This section demonstrates how thoroughly the study of the Scripture had shaped the thought of the authors of the *Confession*.

## Christ's Saving Work

Section four begins the description of the saving work of Jesus as the Messiah. It does so in terms of His humiliation and exaltation, following the pattern of Philippians 2:5-11. He was made subject to the law of God and suffered the penalty for our lawbreaking in His own soul and body, even to death. Because His sacrifice was accepted by the Father, He was raised from the dead, and lifted to the place of supreme honor and authority at His Father's right hand. He now prays for His people, and will return as Judge at the Last Great Day.

The discerning reader will note in this paragraph the influence of the Apostles' Creed, which the Westminster Assembly required parents to recite when they brought their children to be baptized.

The pattern of describing Christ's work as humiliation and exaltation has often been used in the Church for the instruction of converts and the young. It faithfully proclaims the testimony to Christ given in the New Testament, and emphasizes the historical reality of His saving work. It also reminds us that our own pathway to glory leads through the valley of tears (Psalm 84).

## Christ's Suffering and Death

Section five sets forth the biblical doctrine of the atonement. How does the suffering and death of Christ result in our salvation? The *Confession's* answer is that Christ's death on the cross "fully satisfied the justice of the Father." Our sins deserve God's wrath and the penalty of death—eternal separation from God. Christ became our substitute, the sacrificial Lamb of God who took that penalty upon Himself. Because of what He did, we can be forgiven, while God's justice is unimpaired (Rom. 3:24-26). Through His obedience and death, we who were His enemies are reconciled to Him through faith, and are given the sure hope of eternal life.

## Christ's Death and Old Testament Believers

Section six makes the important point that Christ's death was effective for believers who lived before the time Christ died, as well as for those who came afterwards. The atonement was the fulfillment of God's eternal purpose, and therefore it was, so to speak, retroactive. The Scripture makes it clear that the gospel was preached to Abraham, and that those who believed in the Savior who was to come were justified by faith, as we are justified by faith (Rom. 4).

## Christ's Two Natures

Section seven addresses a somewhat technical point related to the truth expressed earlier that the two natures of Christ are distinct from one another. How are we to understand a passage like Acts 20:28, for example, which says that God purchased the church with His own blood? God, being spirit, has no blood, and cannot die. The *Confession*'s answer is that "by reason of the unity of the person, that which is proper to one nature, is sometimes in Scripture attributed to the person denominated (named) by the other nature."

## Christ's Prophetic and Kingly Work

In the first section of this chapter, Christ was said to be Prophet, Priest, and King. His work as Mediator is to be understood as the fulfillment of these three functions. Sections five and six are discussions of His priestly work, in offering sacrifice and making intercession. Section eight speaks of His work as Prophet and King. As Prophet, He reveals to us, in and by the Word, the mysteries (truths known only by revelation) of salvation, and persuades us by His Spirit to believe and obey. As King, He rules our hearts by His Word and Spirit, and protects us from our great adversary, the devil.

The *Confession*'s treatment of Christ's messianic work as Prophet, Priest, and King is not completed in this chapter. Section eight serves as an introduction to the fuller presentation of Christ's work in chapters ten through eighteen.

Neo-orthodox theologians sometimes criticize the *Confession* for not being sufficiently Christ-centered. Such criticisms are without foundation. Chapter eight is a marvelous description of His person and work. Beyond that, the whole application of redemption is here presented as the work of Christ. He calls us to faith by His Spirit, and that faith results in our justification by His righteousness, our adoption into His family, and our sanctification to be conformed to His image. He is the one who preserves us in faith and will make us partakers in His glory. ⊕

# 9

# Do Calvinists Believe in Free Will?

It might seem strange that a strongly Calvinistic document such as the *Westminster Confession of Faith* would include a chapter on free will. Do not Calvinists deny the existence of free will?

The question is not a simple one. Indeed, there has been a long history of philosophical as well as theological debate on the subject. In early Greek philosophy, Democritus and the Stoics denied the existence of free will, while Socrates, Plato, Aristotle, and Epicurus argued for free will. The medieval Roman Catholic theologian Thomas Aquinas contended that the providence of God did not exclude liberty of choice, fortune, or chance (*Summa Contra Gentiles, Book III*, chaps. 63-64).

At the time of the Reformation, Erasmus and Luther had a fierce literary debate over this subject. Erasmus wrote *On Free Will* in 1524, arguing for "the power of the human will whereby man can apply to or turn away from that which leads unto eternal salvation." Luther responded the next year with *The Bondage of the Will*. His position is that "a man devoid of the Spirit of God does not do evil against his will, as though taken by the neck and forced into it,...but he does it spontaneously and willingly. And this willingness and desire of doing evil he cannot, by his own strength, eliminate, restrain, or change. He goes on still desiring and craving to do evil" (*Erasmus-Luther, Discourse on Free Will*, pp.20, 111).

Members of the Westminster Assembly would have been aware of this history of discussion. They included a statement about it in the *Confession* because it has an important bearing on one's view of human need, and of God's grace in the gospel. The *Confession* clearly comes down on Luther's side of the question.

## Human Choice Between Good and Evil

The first section of the chapter states that all human beings possess "natural liberty," that is, man possesses the power of making choices between good and evil. Shakespeare was right when he wrote "To err is human" in reference to human behavior since the Fall. But it is not the case, according to the Bible, that human beings are *essentially* determined toward good or evil. Men and women can change, or, more accurately, they can be changed. Paul wrote to the Corinthians, "Do you not know that the unrighteous will not inherit the kingdom of God?" Then, after listing many kinds of terrible sinners, he continues, "And such *were* [past tense] some of you; but you were washed, but you were sanctified, but you were justified in the name of the Lord Jesus Christ and in the Spirit of our God" (1 Cor. 6:9, 11). It is true that we all choose what we love, but God's grace is able to change what we love. In this way, the will can be changed. The rest of this chapter describes various states or conditions of human existence, in which the will, or the power of choice, operates.

## The State of Innocence

The first is the *state of innocence*, referring to the condition of Adam and Eve before sin came into their lives. They had "freedom and power to will and to do that which was good." The biblical evidence for this is that when God had finished creating the world, including mankind, he declared everything He had made "very good" (Gen. 1:31). Also, the man and woman were created in the image of God, and in chapter 4, the *Confession* declares that the image of God involves "knowledge, righteousness, and true holiness." As human beings, Adam and Eve were making choices as they lived in the garden, and for a time (we don't know how long) they chose to obey God. But their freedom to choose what was good was subject to change, as we know from the account of their disobedience (Gen. 3).

## The State of Sin

The second state is the *state of sin* (section 3). As a sinner, man has lost his former freedom of will. He is not able to choose "any spiritual good accompanying salvation." This does not mean that he no longer has the power of choice, or that he cannot choose to do some things that are comparatively good. Unconverted people often choose to be honest, to be faithful to their marriage vows, to work hard at their vocations, to strive for peace in society, etc. But, being dead in sin (Eph. 2:1, 5), they do not choose the good things that *accompany salvation*. They do not, on their own, love God, or repent of their sins, or put their trust in Christ, or seek to serve Him in all they do. Luther said in *The Bondage of the Will* that man has "free will in respect not of what is above him, but of what is below him...in regard to God and in all things pertaining to salvation or damnation, man has no free will, but is a captive, servant, and bondslave, either to the will of God, or to the will of Satan" (*Discourse*, p. 113). In order to make even the first step toward salvation, sinful men and women need the effectual call of the Spirit, which *renews* the will (see chap. 10).

## The State of Grace

The third state is the *state of grace*. When God gives the new birth, and makes a sinner to be a new creature in Christ, the will is changed, so that now there is the freedom and ability to choose what is *spiritually* good—what God commands, what is well-pleasing to Him. The *Confession* appropriately cites Philippians 2:12-13: "Work out your own salvation with fear and trembling; for it is God who is at work in you, both *to will* and to do his good pleasure." However, the freedom of the will in this state is not complete, for sin still has some power, and sometimes the Christian chooses to do evil. In this life, "If we say that we have no sin, we are deceiving ourselves and the truth is not in us" (1 John 1:8).

## The State of Glory

As we struggle, then, to gain victory over sin, to choose the good, we look forward to the final state, the *state of glory*. "The will of man is made perfectly and immutably free to do good alone in the state of glory only" (9:5). John writes, "Beloved, now we are children of God, and it has not yet appeared what we shall be. We know that, when he appears, we shall be like him, because we shall see him just as he is" (1 John 3:2).

Calvinism does not teach that human beings are robots or puppets, with no power of choice, or that God's sovereignty eliminates human responsibility. The Bible everywhere addresses us as those who make real decisions, and those decisions determine our destiny. But we do not have an absolute freedom of choice. We make our choices according to our nature. Apart from the working of God's grace in our lives, we are hostile to Him and to His law, and will choose accordingly (Rom. 8:7). When God decides to save a sinner, He persuades and enables that person to choose Christ. Behind every true decision to receive Christ is the divine decision, which we call election. God's grace makes us willing, and then we exercise our renewed wills in responding to His gracious invitation. All the glory for our salvation is to Him alone!

# 10

# Powerful, Persuasive, and Personal

The teaching of this chapter builds on what already has been stated in the *Confession of Faith* regarding human need and God's provision through Christ for meeting that need.

In chapter 1:1 it was said that the revelation available to all people through the light of nature and creation is "not sufficient to give that knowledge of God, and of his will, which are necessary for salvation." Chapter 3:3-4 presents the doctrine of God's predestination of some (but not all) men to eternal life "without any foresight of faith or good works." The doctrine of total depravity is set forth in chapter 6:4: by the moral corruption inherited from Adam; "we are utterly indisposed, disabled, and made opposite to all good, and wholly inclined to all evil." The saving work of Christ, according to chapter 8:8, includes not only His obedience, death, and resurrection, but also His communication of redemption to those for whom He died. It is Christ who reveals "unto them, in and by the word, the mysteries of salvation, effectually persuading them by his Spirit to believe and obey; and governing their hearts by his Word and Spirit." In chapter 9, the powerful work of God's grace is seen as overcoming the bondage of sin, as God enables the sinner to do what he otherwise could not do, "freely to will and to do that which is spiritually good." Chapter 10 draws all those strands together to explain how it is that we make the transition from wrath to grace, from the domain of darkness into the kingdom of Christ.

The gracious and powerful work of God by which this comes about is denoted by the *Confession* as "effectual calling." A closely related term is "regeneration," which appears in section 3 of this chapter. When the two terms are used with a different meaning, "effectual calling" refers to God's action, and "regeneration" refers to the effect of that action in the life of the converted sinner. As we seek to summarize the teaching of this chapter, we will discuss (1) the nature of effectual calling, (2) the operation of effectual calling, and (3) the indispensability of effectual calling.

## The Nature of God's Call

Effectual calling is an activity of God that radically changes those who experience it. God calls men and women out of the state, or condition, of sin and death into a state of grace and salvation. Before, they were ignorant of the things of God and of the way to life. When they are called, the light of God shines in their hearts, enabling them to see and understand the truth of God (2 Cor. 4:6; Eph. 4:17-21). Before, they were unresponsive to God and to His Word, dead in trespasses and sins. In the biblical metaphor, they had hearts of stone (Ezek. 11:19-20). In effectual calling, God gives them hearts of flesh, living and responsive to Him (Eph. 1:1-4). Before, their wills were in bondage to sin, as they made decisions in accordance with hearts and minds that were hostile to God (Rom. 8:5-8). In effectual calling, God makes them to be new creatures in Christ, so that their decisions are a reflection of their new nature. In this way, they are drawn to Christ and come to Him freely and gladly (Rom. 6:17-18).

The calling of God is not only powerfully transforming; it is sovereign. God calls those whom He has chosen in Christ before the foundation of the world. The great comfort of Romans 8:29 is that God's saving work is effective in the life of each and every one on whom He has set His love, on each and every one whom He has predestinated to be conformed to the image of His Son. Calling comes to those, and those only, whom He has predestined. It comes in God's "appointed and accepted time." Some are called early in life, even from their mother's womb. Others are saved late in life, like the thief on the cross. Because calling is God's sovereign work, He determines when it shall occur. And calling is sovereign because it is not based on anything in us, "not from anything at all foreseen in man" (Rom. 9:11; 2 Tim. 1:9).

## The Operation of God's Call

In its operation, calling is ordinarily carried out by the Word of God as it is applied to the heart by the Holy Spirit. The *Confession* says in section 1 that God calls "by his word and Spirit." In section 3, special mention is made of those "who are incapable of being outwardly called by the ministry of the word." They include infants who do not survive infancy, and persons who suffer from mental incapacity. Such persons, if they are elect, are saved on the basis of the work of Christ as it is applied to them by the sovereign Holy Spirit.

This, however, is extraordinary. In chapter 14, saving faith is said to be "ordinarily wrought by the ministry of the word." "Faith comes by hearing, and hearing by the word of God" (Rom. 10:17). God usually calls sinners to Himself through the presentation of the truth of the Scripture.

We must apply this doctrine to ourselves by asking whether in our personal lives and in the church we are being diligent to communicate the message of the Scripture to those who do not know Christ. We sometimes speak of friendship evangelism, and indeed we must seek to become acquainted in a friendly way with those who need Christ so that we may have opportunity for witness. But friendship in and of itself will not result in conversion. "How then shall they call on Him of whom they have not believed? And how shall they believe in Him of whom they have not heard?" (Rom. 10:14). Friendship must open the way to sharing the Word of God with those whom we seek to lead to Christ.

For this outward ministry of the Word to be effective, however, it must be driven home to the heart by the Holy Spirit. The writers of the *Confession* were well aware of the fact that many read the Bible, or listen to preaching, yet are unconverted. In a certain sense they are called, but only externally (Matt. 22:14). Hence it must be our continual and fervent prayer that God will bless our efforts in preaching and teaching and witnessing, to make them effective. What brings salvation is not merely knowing the content of the Bible, or being in church, but coming to Christ in faith and repentance.

## The Indispensability of God's Call

Effectual calling—God changing the heart by His Word and Spirit—is indispensable for salvation. The closing words of this chapter contain a position that is very unpopular in our present culture. They assert that salvation comes exclusively by the gospel of Christ, and not by following the light of nature or the tenets of any other religion. Many people today, even those who profess to be Christians, advocate religious pluralism. "There are many paths to God," they say, "and so long as one is sincere in what he believes, all will be well." Almost any pattern of disbelief and practice is tolerated, except that of conservative Christians, who hold to the teaching of Christ: "I am the way, the truth, and the life; no one comes to the Father except through me" (John 14:6). We must not hold to this conviction in a proud way, nor should we be harsh in our dealings with those who hold to other beliefs. We must, however, be faithful to the Scripture, and proclaim with Peter that "there is salvation in no one else; for there is no other name under heaven that has been given among men by which we must be saved" (Acts 4:12).   ⊕

# 11

## Pardon and Acceptance

Martin Luther called the doctrine of justification "the article by which the church stands or falls." When he discovered in the Scriptures the good news that sinners are justified by trusting in Christ and His righteousness, he found the peace with God for which he had been searching desperately. As others came to share his discovery, the result was the Protestant Reformation. The motto of the Reformation was "salvation by grace alone, through faith in Christ alone."

The Reformation focus on justification is the background for this chapter in the *Confession of Faith*; here the Reformation motto sounds forth clearly.

### Justification

The first section summarizes the teaching of Scripture on justification. There are two aspects involved in the justification of sinners: God's "pardoning their sins" and God's "accounting and accepting their persons as righteous." Both of these actions are judicial declarations by God as Judge. When a judge condemns a lawbreaker, he does not change the moral character of that person, but declares how the person stands in relation to the law and its penalties. Likewise, justifying a person produces no moral change; it is a pronouncement about his standing before the law.

## Christ Alone

These two aspects of justification are based upon two aspects of Christ's saving work that are mentioned several times in this chapter. Our forgiveness is based on Christ's satisfaction; our being counted as (positively) righteous is based on His perfect fulfillment of the law of God on our behalf. This is more fully explained in the third section: "Christ, by his obedience and death, did fully discharge the debt of all those that are thus justified, and did make a proper, real, and full satisfaction to his Father's justice in their behalf." If we speak of this in covenant terms, we may say that by His life Christ fulfilled the requirement of the Covenant of Works, "personal, perfect and perpetual obedience," and thus gained for those whom He represented the life promised in the covenant. By His suffering, He took upon Himself the penalty prescribed in that covenant, namely, death, so that we are delivered from it. (See the *Westminster Larger Catechism*, Question 20.) These words present the basis, or ground, of justification, which is the work and merit of Christ alone. Here we hear one of the watchwords of the Reformation, *solo Christo*, by "Christ alone."

One effective way of clarifying the truth of Scripture is by contrasting it with what is false. The *Confession* does so in this first section. Justification is not by infusion of righteousness into a person, thereby changing his character. Rather, it is the imputation of Christ's obedience and satisfaction, as God reckons them to our account, as though we had performed them (see Phil. 3:9). Justification is not based on anything in us—not on anything we do, not on our faith or obedience, and not even on anything that God produces in us. Even the faith by which we receive justification is not our own doing; it is the gift of God.

## Faith Alone

The second section of the chapter concentrates on the instrument, or means, by which we are justified—that is, faith alone. As in chapter 4, saving faith is here described as "receiving and resting on Christ, and His righteousness." This is in harmony with the Reformed understanding of faith, as having three elements: knowledge, assent, and trust. To be saved, we need to know the meaning of the gospel, to be persuaded that it is true, and then to act upon what we believe by entrusting ourselves to Christ. The sequence of questions in Romans 10:13-15 supports this view of faith: hearing the gospel leads to believing, and believing leads to calling upon the Lord. In this section, we hear again the Reformation cry, *sola fide*, "by faith alone."

At the time of the Reformation, the Roman Catholics charged that to teach justification by faith alone would lead to careless and immoral living. The reply of the Reformers was that while "faith alone saves, the faith which saves is never alone." We hear that answer echoed here: faith is "the alone instrument of justification, yet it is not alone in the person justified, but is ever accompanied with all other saving graces, and is no dead faith, but worketh by love." Roman Catholic doctrine merges justification and sanctification. In the Reformed view, they are quite distinct (see *Larger Catechism*, Question 77), but cannot be separated. Those whom God justifies, He also sanctifies. Our thankfulness for being forgiven and accepted by God becomes powerful motivation for a life of godliness, and He gives us His Spirit in order that we may bear the fruit of righteousness (Gal. 5:22-23). Where the gospel of free grace is most clearly preached and believed, there concern for true godliness is most clearly seen.

## Grace Alone

In the latter part of the third section, the graciousness of justification is highlighted. The Father was not obligated to give His Son for our salvation; He did so out of His free grace. God was not bound to accept the work of Christ on our behalf; He did so freely. Thus His "rich grace" is abundantly evident in the way in which He justifies sinners. Here we hear the third of the "alone" words of the Reformation: *sola gratia*, "by grace alone." (The fourth, *sola Scriptura*, "based on Scripture alone," has already been expressed in chapter 1 of the *Confession*.)

## The Plan of Justification Before and After Christ

Two smaller, but still important, issues are covered in sections 4 and 6. According to the fourth section, justification occurs in time, after a person believes. There was a time for each believer when he or she was a "child of wrath" (Eph. 2:3). We are justified by faith, and therefore not before we believe. To be sure, our justification is in God's plan (Rom. 8:29-30), but it is important to distinguish between the plan and the fulfillment of the plan; otherwise, human history and human responsibility have no meaning.

In the sixth section, the *Confession* makes the point that the justification of God's Old Testament people was essentially the same as that of those who live after the cross. Paul can therefore appeal to Abraham as the great biblical example of being justified by faith (see Rom. 4; Gal. 3). David sang of justification in Psalm 32. Luther's liberating text, "The just shall live by faith," comes from Habakkuk 2:4.

## Forgiveness

The fifth section addresses a perplexing question: If we are justified, once and for all, when we believe in Christ, why do we need to continue to ask for forgiveness, as we are instructed to do in the Lord's Prayer? The *Confession*'s answer is that we never lose our justification. When we sin, however, our fellowship with our heavenly Father is disturbed. We suffer His "fatherly displeasure," and we may experience the "chastening" that is an expression of His love (Heb. 12:5-11). When our own children disobey, the peace and joy of the relationship are diminished, until there is an acknowledgement of wrong on the child's part. When that comes, how glad we are to grant the forgiveness that is asked! In the meantime, the disobedient child is still loved, is still part of the family. So it is in our relationship with our Father in heaven.

## Searching the Scriptures

On the 480<sup>th</sup> anniversary of Luther's posting of the 95 theses that began the Protestant Reformation, representatives of the Roman Catholic and some Lutheran churches signed a document titled, "A Joint Declaration on the Doctrine of Justification." The press heralded this event as if it brought to an end the centuries-long division between these two bodies. We should rejoice in any step that is taken to lessen the divisions among Christians, provided that such a step does not represent the abandonment or obscuring of the truth of the gospel. The document in question is long and complex (in the copy I have seen, seven closely spaced pages, with 44 sections). There does seem to be an agreement that justification is based on grace and the work of Christ, and not on human merit. However, there are many troubling features. The churches do not disavow their past statements on justification (this calls for careful study of the Catholics' Canons and Decrees of the Council of Trent, and the Lutherans' Formula of Concord). Justification is said to be received through the Sacrament of Baptism, and sins committed subsequent to baptism cannot be forgiven except through the Sacrament of Reconciliation (Penance). The possibility of having assurance of salvation is not clearly affirmed; instead, it is said that believers "may be certain that God intends their salvation" (section 36).

Christians must continue to follow in the footsteps of Luther in searching the Scriptures to discover the only way in which a sinner can be declared just before God. This chapter of the *Confession* will assist us in identifying the issues that need to be addressed, and will point us to the biblical passages in which the nature, basis, and means of justification are made clear. Taking the Scripture as the only rule of faith and life, we confess that justification is indeed by grace alone, based on the work of Christ alone, received through faith alone. Salvation is of the Lord. To Him alone be the glory!

# 12

## Undeserving Heirs

Among the major Reformed confessions, the *Westminster Confession of Faith* is the only one that devotes a separate chapter to the subject of adoption. The others, if they mention adoption at all, treat it as part of justification.

We may be grateful that the Westminster documents emphasize this aspect of our salvation, because many passages of Scripture speak of the blessed privileges that are ours as the sons and daughters of God. More than half of this brief chapter of the *Confession* is made of expressions taken directly from Scripture.

### Adoption and Justification

Adoption resembles justification in that, in human practice, both involve legal processes. Justification is the pronouncement of a judge or a court that a person is not liable to penalties for violating the law, or, positively, that a person has met the obligations of the law. Adoption involves a legal pronouncement that a person who is not a child by birth now possesses all the rights and responsibilities of a son or daughter in the adopting family. In Greek culture, adoption usually involved the making of a new will by the adoptive parents, so that the one who was adopted immediately became an heir of the family.

Adoption differs from justification in that it is drawn from our experience of what it is to be part of a family. It is one thing for a judge to pronounce an accused person "not guilty." It would be an amazing thing if the judge then invited the acquitted person to come home with him and be a member of his family. Yet that is what God has done for us in Christ!

## "Vouchsafeth"

The *Confession* emphasizes the graciousness of God in making us His children by adoption, by using the old word "vouchsafeth." This interesting word combines a number of different meanings. It means to grant, or give, something, and so makes the point that we receive adoption as a gift. We are not by nature the children of God; by nature we are "children of disobedience," "children of wrath" (Eph. 2:2-3). While many reject Christ, "as many as received Him, to them He gave the right to become children of God, even to those who believe on His name" (John 1:12).

"Vouchsafeth" also has in it the idea of condescension, so it expresses the fact that God was under no obligation to make us His children, but did it out of His unmerited love. The *Confession* strengthens this idea by its reference to "the grace of adoption."

A third meaning contained in "vouchsafeth" is the idea of a warrant, or a guarantee. We sometimes speak of "vouching" for another person, that is, we testify to his identity or reliability. So, in our adoption, God gives His word that we are His own dear children, bearing witness to that fact in our hearts by His Holy Spirit (Rom. 8:16-17).

## Adoption and Justification Work Together

While justification and adoption can be distinguished from one another, they cannot be separated. The *Confession* says, "All those who are justified" and made "partakers of the grace of adoption." Both justification and adoption come to us when we believe in Christ. Paul wrote to the Galatians, "Therefore the Law has become our tutor to lead us to Christ, so that we may be justified by faith. For you are all sons of God through faith in Christ Jesus" (Gal. 3:24, 26).

Adoption comes to us as a result of Christ's redeeming work, "in and for [God's] only Son Jesus Christ." It is one of the benefits of our union with Christ. "He predestined us to adoption as sons through Jesus Christ" (Eph. 1:5).

## Adoption and Where It Leads

The *Confession* first describes adoption in general terms, and then gives a number of specific statements drawn from Scripture. The general statement is, "They are taken into the number, and enjoy the liberties and privileges of the children of God." It is likely that, when the authors of the *Confession* used the word "liberties," they meant it as a synonym of the word "privileges." They did not cite a prooftext for this statement that had in it the idea of freedom. Yet we should note that the Scripture does connect our sonship with freedom. Paul makes that point in Galatians. He declares that Christ came into the world "in order that He might redeem those who were under the Law, that we might receive the adoption as sons" (Gal. 4:5). He goes on to say that, because God now deals with us as sons, we are no longer under the ceremonial laws of the Old Testament. He concludes: "It is for freedom that Christ set you free; therefore keep standing firm, and do not be subject again to a yoke of slavery" (5:1). There is a fuller discussion of that freedom we have in Christ in chapter 20 of the *Confession*.

Chapter 12 concludes by giving a list of our liberties and privileges as children of God. The phrases that make up the list do not require much explanation. It will be profitable to meditate on the Scripture passages that are given in support of each phrase.

### Prayer

It is worth commenting that the *Confession* treats adoption as a strong encouragement to prayer. Because we are adopted as children, we "have access to the throne of grace with boldness, [and] are enabled to cry, Abba, Father." We need to remember, then, that Jesus instructed us to pray to our Father in heaven. The *Larger Catechism* (Q. 189) says that we are thus instructed, "when we pray, to draw near to God with confidence of his fatherly goodness, and our interest therein, with reverence, and all other child-like dispositions." Understanding the doctrine of adoption will help us to pray in the right way, confident of the love of our heavenly Father.

## Fellowship

The doctrine of adoption speaks not only of our vertical relationship to God, but of our relationship to our brothers and sisters in Christ. Perhaps the *Confession* intends to give this perspective when it speaks of our being "received into the number" of the children of God. One of the biblical metaphors for the Church is that of the "household of God" (Eph. 2:19). To be received as the sons and daughters of God is to become a member of the Church. Chapter 26, "Of the Communion of Saints," presents a beautiful picture of what it means to live as a member of the family of God: "And being united to one another in love, they have communion in each others' gifts and graces."

In an issue of the American *Reformed Presbyterian Witness*, there is a beautiful testimony of God's grace from a young woman who was rescued by Christ from a life of addiction, homelessness, and immorality. She came to faith in Christ and then found fellowship in an RP Church in New York. "The church became a special family to me," she writes. "I also saw that being in the church protected me from the negative influences around me, and gave me a place to grow spiritually."

As we seek to minister in a world where people often experience abandonment and alienation from their natural families, we can proclaim the gospel that offers acceptance into the family of God, our loving heavenly Father. As the Church, we are the family of God in which those who become

His sons and daughters can experience His love, protection, and provision.

As we study this chapter of the *Confession*, may we share John's exclamation of amazement and hope: "See how great a love the Father has bestowed upon us, that we should be called the children of God; and such we are. Beloved, now we are the children of God, and it has not as yet appeared what we shall be. We know that, when He appears, we shall be like Him, because we shall see Him just as He is" (1 John 3:1-2).

# 13

# Your Progress in Holiness

This chapter is part of the *Westminster Confession of Faith's* presentation of the benefits purchased by Christ by His obedient life and sacrificial death for His people.

In preparation for this reflection on the chapter's contents, it is suggested that you read through it. What strikes you? What resonates most with your own experience? For some, I expect, it will be the negative statements of the chapter: Sanctification is "imperfect in this life...there abideth still some remnants of corruption in every part: whence ariseth a continual and irreconcilable war." Commentators on the *Confession* always give arguments against perfectionism as they deal with this chapter. In Reformed circles, there often seems to be a spirit of pessimism about progress in holiness.

## Struggling toward Holiness

The *Confession* is soundly biblical when it asserts the fact that Christians are not perfect in this life. "If we say that we have no sin, we are deceiving ourselves and the truth is not in us" (1 John 1:8). A struggle against sin is indeed our ongoing experience. However, awareness of our imperfection should not blind us to the great encouragement of the Scripture about God's provision for our progress in holiness. As Peter writes, God's "divine power has granted to us everything pertaining to life and godliness, through the true knowledge of Him who called us by His own glory and excellence. For by these He has granted to us His precious and magnificent promises, so that by them you might become partakers of the divine nature, having escaped the corruption that is in the world by lust" (2 Pet. 1:3-4). That encouragement is clearly presented in the *Confession*'s discussion of sanctification.

The term sanctification means "separation." It is used in Scripture of someone or something being set apart to the worship and service of God, and also of being separated from impurity and sin. Here it is used in the latter sense: Believers are sanctified "really and personally." In justification, our legal standing is changed, as we are counted righteous before God, not for our own righteousness, but for the righteousness of Christ. In sanctification, we are changed in our moral character; we are made new creatures in Christ (2 Cor. 5:17). (See *Larger Catechism*, Q. 77, for a statement of the differences between justification and sanctification.)

The *Confession* describes this change both negatively and positively. Negatively, "the dominion of the whole body of sin is destroyed, and the several lusts thereof are more and more weakened and mortified." Positively, believers are "more and more quickened [enlivened, stimulated] and strengthened in all saving graces." The phrase "body of sin" is taken from Romans 6:6. It is likely that the Assembly understood its meaning as Thomas Manton, an English Puritan of the same period, did—as "the whole mass and stock of corruption," not the physical body. In the life of a believer, sin no longer dominates. The tendency to sinful life diminishes, and the inclination to a righteous and holy life increases.

It is interesting that the *Confession* presents sanctification as the continuation of a process already begun: "They who are effectually called and regenerated, having a new heart and a new spirit created in them, are further sanctified." This recalls the chapter on effectual calling, which described a decisive change of nature, involving the mind, heart, and will. What was begun in effectual calling is continued in sanctification.

## Desiring Holiness

This teaching of the *Confession* has been developed in different terms by Professor John Murray in his distinction between "definitive" and "progressive" sanctification. Murray describes definitive sanctification in these words: "For every believer in Jesus...there is the decisive and irreversible breach with the world and with its defilement and power.... The person begotten of God does righteousness, loves and knows God, loves those who are begotten of God, and keeps the commandments of God" (1 John 2:3-6, 29; 4:7, 20-21; 5:2-3) (*Collected Writings*, 2, 283-4).

If this decisive change has not taken place, if there is no desire for practical holiness, then there is a real question whether or not a person has been genuinely converted. Sanctification differs from justification, but they can never be separated. Whom God justifies, He also sanctifies.

That break with sin, though real and radical, is not yet complete; and so there is the continuing work of progressive sanctification, which is the focus of this chapter of the *Confession*. Sinful desires are "more and more" weakened; the graces that are the fruit of the Spirit are "more and more" quickened and strengthened. This growth in grace, in the view of the *Confession*, is to be a lifelong process.

## Holiness through Christ Alone

The *Confession*, following the Scriptures, traces sanctification to its source—"through virtue of Christ's death and resurrection." The word *virtue* has the sense of power. (In the English of the King James Version, Jesus felt *virtue* go out of Him when the woman who touched His garment was healed.) What is being asserted here is that sanctification is the outcome of the saving work of Christ. This ought to be of great encouragement to us in our efforts to make progress in holiness: Christ died and rose again so that we might be holy. As we are united to Him by faith, the power of His death and resurrection is realized in our lives.

The Holy Spirit who dwells in us is the Person of the Godhead who particularly accomplishes our sanctification. He is the "Spirit of holiness." As we live and walk in the Spirit, we are transformed, and the fruit of the Spirit—love, joy, peace, patience, etc.—become evident in our lives.

## Scripture as a Means of Holiness

The *Confession* points to the Word of God as the means by which we are sanctified. It has in mind the prayer of Jesus to His Father: "Sanctify them in the truth; Your Word is truth" (John 17:17). No doubt reference could be made to the other means of grace, as most commentators do, but the *Confession* focuses on the Word. In the next chapter, on saving faith, we learn that the Word is a means of grace as we respond to it in faith, "yielding obedience to the commands, trembling at the threatenings, and embracing the promises of God." Progress in sanctification comes as the Spirit enables us to respond to the Scripture in such practical and experiential ways.

In reflecting on this chapter, something seems to be missing. When the Scripture speaks of our growth in holiness, it places great emphasis on our effort, our active involvement. First Peter, for example, places great emphasis on holiness. "You shall be holy, for I am holy" (1:16). In this epistle, there are a great many commands and exhortations that call for our response. We are to "gird our minds for action"; "fervently love one another"; "abstain from fleshly lusts," "keep [our] behavior excellent"; "be harmonious, sympathetic, brotherly, kindhearted, and humble in spirit"; "turn away from evil and do good," etc. The *Confession*, however, seems to concentrate on what *God* does in our sanctification; most of the verbs in the chapter are passive.

It is certainly not the intention of the *Confession* to say that Christians are entirely passive in sanctification. In the

*Shorter Catechism*, Q. 35, sanctification is described as "the work of God's free grace, whereby we are enabled more and more to die unto sin and live unto righteousness." God does the enabling, but we are the ones who do the dying unto sin and living unto righteousness. The way in which God's work and ours are brought together in sanctification is found in Philippians 2:12-13: "Work out your salvation with fear and trembling; for it is God who is at work in you, both to will and to work for His good pleasure." The only reason that we desire to be holy, and bend our efforts in that direction is because God is working in us. But if He is working in us, then we will vigorously pursue holiness.

There are many wrong notions about holiness in the church. Some say that personal holiness is not necessary in a believer's life. To them we say, with the Scripture and the *Confession*, that without holiness "no one will see the Lord" (Heb. 12:14). Some teach that holiness may be achieved by our own efforts, without the grace of God and the work of the Spirit in our lives. To them we say, with the Scripture and the *Confession*, it is by the Word and Spirit of God, based on the death and resurrection of Christ, that we are sanctified (2 Thess. 2:13). Some are very discouraged about progress in holiness, because they are conscious of weakness and remaining sin in their lives. We say to them (and to ourselves), "through the continual supply of strength from the sanctifying Spirit of Christ" Christians may, and Christians do, "grow in grace, perfecting holiness in the fear of God."

# 14

## Saving Faith is a Living Faith

Chapters 7 and 18 of the *Confession* present various aspects of the doctrine of salvation. Until the present chapter, the emphasis is on what God does objectively to save us from our sins, and from the penalty of death we deserve. With chapter 14, and the two following chapters, the focus changes to our subjective response to God's saving work. We begin with "Saving Faith."

### Defining Saving Faith

The term "saving faith" is used because we learn from Scripture and experience that there are kinds of faith that do not save. The demons believe that there is one God, but are not saved (Jas. 2:19). The religious leaders who sought to kill Jesus had confidence that the Scriptures told of the way to eternal life, but refused to come to Jesus as the One in whom alone such life is to be found (John 5:38-40). Since not all faith is saving faith, it is essential for us to know what the Bible teaches about the kind of faith that results in salvation.

Saving faith is not something we ourselves create by an act of will. It is the "grace" of faith, a result of God's unmerited favor (Eph. 2:8-9). Those God has chosen in His sovereign grace to receive salvation are enabled to do what they could not do in their own strength—that is, to "believe to the saving of their souls." The *Confession* is here following the teaching of Jesus recorded in John: "No one can come to me unless the Father who sent me draws him....All that the Father gives me shall come to me" (John 6:44, 37).

### Receiving Saving Faith

The ability to believe is given by the working of the Holy Spirit in a person's heart and mind. Faith is part of the fruit of the Spirit described in Galatians 5:22-23. When Paul preached to the women gathered by the riverside for prayer near Philippi, the Lord opened Lydia's heart, and she believed (Acts 16:14). So it is with everyone who has saving faith.

The Lord ordinarily uses means to accomplish His work, and in giving us faith He uses the Word. "Faith comes by hearing, and hearing by the Word of Christ" (Rom. 10:17). Faith is not a vague, mystical experience, but is believing the truth God has given us in His Word. Reading the Bible, participating in Bible studies with others, and listening to the preaching of the gospel are the ways in which people most often come to true faith in Christ. Because of this, the Bible must have a central place in the lives of God's people, and in the church.

There is a church in Pittsburgh, Pa., that attracts large numbers of people by using drama and contemporary Christian music. At the service on the Lord's Day, this church often has no sermon; sometimes there is no Scripture reading. Such a church may have a large attendance, but it is doubtful that, by such a program, many will come to a saving knowledge of Christ.

### Living Faith

Saving faith is a living faith. Believing in Christ marks the beginning of the Christian life, but faith does not end there. The *Confession* speaks of faith being increased and strengthened by the use of all the means of grace: the Word, sacraments, and prayer. The means of grace are found within the church, so new believers should be encouraged to become a part of the church as soon as possible. Under the instruction of pastors and teachers, and through the ministry of other Christians, we will all make progress toward attaining "the unity of the faith and of the knowledge of the Son of God, to a mature man, to the measure of the stature that belongs to the fullness of Christ" (Eph. 4:11-13).

## Saving Faith in Action

The second section of the chapter describes saving faith in action, first in a general way, and then more specifically. In its most general terms, faith may be defined as responding rightly to the Word of God. Genuine faith involves accepting the whole teaching of the Bible as true. This is because, as was stated in the first chapter of the *Confession*, God Himself is the author of the Bible. If we believe in God, we will also believe that He has spoken the truth when He gave us the words of the Bible. Jesus prayed to His Father, "Sanctify them in Thy truth; Thy word is truth" (John 17:17). The high view of the doctrine of inspiration held by the Westminster Assembly comes to expression here.

### Responding to God's Word

Beyond this general acceptance of the Bible as true, the *Confession* then describes more specifically what responding rightly to the Word of God involves. Not all the passages of the Bible are alike, and different passages require different responses. Commands require obedience; threatenings require trembling; promises need to be embraced. Saving faith is experiential; it is active; it involves our whole being, as we respond to God's Word.

Reflect on your own response to God's Word. Are you more than a hearer? Do you ever tremble? Do you cling to its promises as a drowning woman might cling to a life preserver? We must do more than profess to believe the Bible "from cover to cover." We must live "by every word that proceeds out of the mouth of God" (Matt. 4:4).

## "Accepting Christ"

Even more specifically: Saving faith means "accepting, receiving, and resting upon Christ alone for justification, sanctification, and eternal life, by virtue of the covenant of grace." Some Calvinists are uncomfortable about using the phrase "accepting Christ." They fear that such language puts too much emphasis on human decision with regard to salvation. The *Confession*, however, is not afraid to speak of accepting Christ. Already the truth has been emphasized that faith is the fruit of election and is God's gracious gift. When God's Spirit works savingly in a person's heart, however, He does not believe for that person, but "persuades and enables" him or her to believe. We should not tell people that they are to remain passive when they hear the gospel. Like the apostles, we are to urge them to repent and believe.

Salvation is a gift we are to receive. Christ is the Savior on whom we are to rest. By His miraculous birth, His sinless life, His sacrificial death, and His glorious resurrection, He has accomplished all that was needed for our salvation. He has provided not only for our forgiveness, but also for our real holiness, and for our future glorification. We may safely entrust ourselves to Him for time and eternity.

## Strengthened Faith

The third section of the chapter acknowledges that our faith is often weak. Our salvation, however, does not depend on the strength of our faith. It has often been said that faith is the hand by which we receive God's gift of salvation. Even a weak hand can receive life-giving food or medicine. And if we feel that we are entirely unable to believe, we should remember the man with the withered hand whom Jesus healed. He was truly helpless; but when Jesus said, "Stretch out your hand!" he received strength to respond (Matt. 12:13).

The concluding thought of the chapter is that, though our faith may be weak, Christ, the author and finisher of faith, will enable us to be victorious in faith, and lead us to full assurance. That assurance is more fully discussed in Chapter 18. ⊕

# 15

## Real Repentance, Real Life

This chapter on repentance, along with the chapter on saving faith (Chap. 14), shows that the *Westminster Confession* is deeply evangelical; that is, its focus is on Christ and salvation. In general, the *Confession* follows the outline of Calvin's *Institutes of the Christian Religion*, which has four parts, three of them having to do with our salvation ("The Knowledge of God the Creator"; "The Knowledge of God the Redeemer in Christ"; "The Way in which We Receive the Grace of Christ"; "The External Means . . . by which God Invites Us into the Society of Christ and Holds Us Therein").

Chapters 14 and 15 of the *Confession* seek to make clear how sinners such as ourselves may receive the great salvation purchased by Christ: by faith and repentance.

### Repentance and Gospel Preaching

The doctrine of repentance is thus presented in section 1 as a part of gospel preaching. Repentance is an evangelical grace, flowing from God's unmerited favor, a gift of His love. Previous chapters on sin and effectual calling have made it clear from the Bible that we are unwilling and unable to turn to God on our own. In His sovereign grace, He grants the gift of repentance to those He is drawing into a saving relationship with Christ (Acts 11:18).

It is good for us to be reminded of the emphasis given to repentance in the Bible. In Luke's version of the Great Commission, Christ's command is that "repentance for forgiveness of sins should be proclaimed in His name to all nations, beginning from Jerusalem" (Luke 24:47). J. I. Packer has described popular Christianity in our time as "hot-tub religion," in which the great desire is to feel comfortable. The preaching of repentance does not fit this kind of religion, but it is an essential part of the gospel.

## Biblical Repentance

The second section of the chapter contains a description of biblical repentance. The various biblical terms for repentance mean "a change of mind," "sorrow," "regret," and "turning" (Jer. 8:4-6; Matt. 21:28-32; Acts 26:20; 1 Kings 8:35, 47; 1 Thess. 1:9-10). The *Confession* follows Scripture in teaching that repentance has elements of knowledge, emotion, and decision. Repentance means seeing or understanding the danger of judgment to which our sin exposes us, and realizing that our sins are in opposition to God's holy nature and law. Before regeneration, we don't understand the sinfulness of sin, but when God opens our spiritual eyes we are made aware of our guilt and helplessness before God. The preaching of repentance, therefore, means preaching the requirements and penalties of the law of God.

But repentance is more than understanding; it involves an appropriate emotional response. We come to have a sense of our sins, to grieve for them, and to hate them. This was Paul's experience, described in Romans 7:18-25. True awareness of sin and the revulsion this produces lead to the third element of repentance, which is decision, or action: "turning from them all to God" with the intention of living differently (1 Thess. 1:9-10).

This will, perhaps, strike the reader as familiar and accepted teaching. But we need to ask whether repentance of this kind is part of our Christian experience. Do preachers of the gospel expect to see true grief being expressed as their hearers respond? Are there any tears? Would we be embarrassed or scandalized if brokenness of spirit were to be expressed in our assemblies? Do we weep in private for our sins?

The repentance described here is inseparable from faith in Christ. What would motivate a sinner, conscious of the odiousness of sin, to turn to God, the Holy One whose "eyes are too pure to approve evil" (Hab. 1:12-13)? Only the knowledge of His mercy in Christ. John Murray has written of the interdependence of faith and repentance: "Faith is faith in Christ for salvation from sin. But if faith is directed to salvation from sin, there must be hatred of sin and the desire to be saved from it. Such hatred of sin involves . . . turning from sin unto God. Again, if we remember that repentance is turning from sin unto God, the turning to God implies faith in the mercy of God as revealed in Christ" (*Redemption Accomplished and Applied*, p. 113).

Some of the later Puritans believed that a person had to go through a period of preparation, a time of "law-work" and conviction for sin, before he or she was ready to hear the gospel and come to Christ for salvation. The perspective of the *Confession* is that the preaching of the law and of the gospel must go together, and that faith and repentance are two sides of the experience of conversion.

## Repentance, Not Penance

The third section of the chapter makes the point that, while repentance is necessary for salvation, it does not merit salvation. This is a rejection of the doctrine of penance, which holds that forgiveness of sin requires contrition, confession to a priest, satisfaction, and absolution. The "satisfaction" is some painful work imposed by the priest to satisfy divine justice as a condition of forgiveness. The *Confession* here echoes the teaching in the chapter on justification (Chap. 11), that the finished work of Christ is the only basis for our forgiveness; salvation is by grace alone. Repentance and faith are like the signature on a check, having no value of their own, but only serving as the means or instrument by which the treasure of salvation comes to us.

## Encouragement to Repent

In its evangelical concern, the *Confession* in section 4 brings encouragement to those who feel the greatness of their sin and guilt: "There is no sin so great, that it can bring damnation upon those who truly repent." The Apostle Paul called himself the "chief of sinners"; he was deeply conscious of the fact that he had been a persecutor of Christians before he met God (1 Tim. 1:12-15). Knowing that he had been forgiven, he was able to proclaim to others the glorious gospel of salvation to the worst of sinners.

It is relatively easy for us to acknowledge that we are sinners in a general way. "Nobody's perfect" falls easily from our lips. But the *Confession* makes the point that we need to be specific in our repentance: We are to repent of "particular sins particularly." There is a balance needed here. John Calvin warns us against being thoughtless as we confess our sins: "Now what do we account more hateful . . . to God than the fiction of someone asking pardon for all sins, all the while either thinking he is not a sinner, or at least not thinking he is a sinner?" (*Institutes*, III 20:6).

There is need for balance. We should not be like Luther before his conversion, when he wearied his confessor by seeking to deal with every single instance of sin that he could bring to mind, and then came again immediately to confess the inadequacy of his confession! On the other hand, we should seek to measure our lives by the Scriptures as we study them and hear them preached, and seek forgiveness for those sins the Spirit brings to our minds. I have found it helpful in this regard to use the exposition of the Ten Commandments in the *Catechism*, along with the proof texts, to guide in self-examination.

## Confession of Sin

The final section of the chapter deals with the place of confession of sin. True repentance will lead to confession of sin (1 John 1:9-10). Since Christ is our only mediator, confession is to be made to God through Him alone (Heb. 4:14-16). Beyond that, there is a place for confession of sins to those we have hurt and offended by our sin so that reconciliation can take place (Matt. 5:23-24; 18:15). Depending on the sin, that confession may be private or public. (For a biblical and very practical presentation of how we should deal with offenses and conflict in the church, read *The Peacemaker* by Ken Sande.)

Continuing the evangelical thrust of this chapter, the *Confession* declares that, when appropriate confession has taken place, those offended are to be reconciled to the sinner, and, in love, to receive him. In a little known document of the Westminster Assembly, the *Directory of Government*, there is a beautiful description of how one who has been under church discipline and has repented is to be received by the church: "He is to be pronounced in the name of Christ absolved and free from the censures of the church, and declared to have right to all the ordinances of Christ, with praising of God for His grace, and prayer that he may be fully accepted to His favor, and hear joy and gladness....After this sentence of absolution, the minister speaketh to him as a brother, exhorting him to watch and pray, or comforting him if there be need; the elders embrace him, and the whole congregation holdeth communion with him as one of their own."

When such events occur, it is seen that genuine repentance is truly "repentance unto life."

# 16

## Of Good Works

In unfolding the teaching of Scripture about salvation, the *Confession of Faith* has six chapters that focus on what God does to save us, followed by four chapters on our activity and responsibility in responding to His grace.

The chapters that emphasize what we do are those on saving faith, repentance unto life, good works, and the perseverance of the saints. As will be seen in the discussion of good works, the gracious activity of God and the responsible activity of men and women are never separated.

The Westminster Assembly devoted a chapter to good works for two reasons: (1) This was the subject of very strong controversy between Roman Catholic doctrine and the teaching of the Reformation; and (2) The Scripture refers very frequently to "good works." The latter expression is found 23 times in the New Testament (in the *King James Version*), and there are many other places where the relationship between "works" and our salvation is set forth.

The subject of good works is still very important for us. It has been our experience in seeking to present the gospel that most people, when asked about their hope for going to be with God in heaven when they die, will give some kind of "works" response: "I am a church member." "I am basically a good person." "I try to practice the Golden Rule."

On the other hand, there is a very popular kind of "Christian" teaching today that asserts one may be saved simply by assenting to the truth that Jesus died for sinners, without repentance from sin or commitment to a life of obedience to Christ.

The solid biblical viewpoint of this chapter will help guard us against both kinds of error.

## What Good Works Are

First the *Confession* gives guidance as to what kind of activity is meant by "good works." They are not duties or actions designed or prescribed by human thought or authority, however well intentioned, but only "such as God hath commanded in His holy Word." This is an expression, in the sphere of ethics, of the Reformation principle that Scripture alone is the rule for our salvation, faith, and life. God said to His people long ago, "You shall not add to the word which I am commanding you, nor take away from it" (Deut. 4:2). Jesus rebuked the religious leaders of His day, because "In vain they do worship me, teaching as doctrines the commandments of men" (Matt. 15:9). Since Scripture is the sufficient rule for our faith and life, we may not require of ourselves or others anything that Scripture does not require.

## Why We Do Good Works

The purposes for which we are to do those things that God's Word commands (good works) are set forth in the second section. These works of obedience give evidence that our faith in Christ is genuine. This is what James taught: Faith without works is dead; that is, it is not faith at all (Jas. 2:18-22). The faith that saves is a faith that works by love (Gal. 5:6). Thus, good works in believers' lives strengthen their assurance of salvation.

Works are the means by which we show our thankfulness for God's grace. Both the *Heidelberg Catechism* (Q. 86) and the *Westminster Larger Catechism* (Q. 97) present obedience to the Law of God as the way in which we show our gratitude for God's grace in Christ.

Our good works are helpful to others. They edify our brothers and sisters in Christ by ministering to their needs, and by encouraging them in their efforts to walk with the Lord. Our works are important in evangelism, as they "adorn the profession of the gospel," and refute the accusations of opponents. It is said that Charles Spurgeon was once challenged to a public debate by a society of atheists in London. After they had brought their rationalistic arguments against Christianity, Spurgeon replied by asking how many charitable institutions had been established by their organization. They could name none. Then, he enumerated many such works done in the name of Christ. Recalling Elijah's contest with the prophets of Baal on Mt. Carmel, he cried, "The God who answers by orphanages, let him be God!"

Good works glorify God, and, as evidence of true faith, lead to eternal life (Phil. 1:11; Rom. 6:22).

## God's Help in Good Works

The third section presents the careful balance between God's activity and ours in the performance of good works. On one hand, we must constantly realize that, apart from God's daily working in us by His Spirit, we can do nothing that is truly good (John 15:5). On the other hand, we are not to be merely passive, waiting for God to move us to obedience. Scripture is filled with urgent demands that we consciously and willingly respond to God's revealed will.

The proper balance is found in Philippians 2:12-13, whose words are incorporated in this section: "Work out your salvation with fear and trembling; for it is God who is at work in you, both to will and to work for His good pleasure." Jerry Bridges has written in a very helpful way about this balance between relying on the grace of God while practicing spiritual discipline in his book, *Trusting God* (NavPress).

## Surplus Good Works?

The fourth section reflects a dispute with Roman Catholic teaching concerning the possibility of doing so-called "works of supererogation"—that is, of not only performing all that God requires, but more, so that there is a surplus of merit derived from the saints that is made available to others through the sacraments. While holding out the promise of real progress in holiness (in the chapter on sanctification), the *Confession* also asserts that our obedience will always fall short of what it should be. This is the teaching of 1 John. In that letter, John strongly teaches that the new birth radically changes our nature, so that we do not continually and habitually sin, but are enabled to obey and to love. At the same time, he writes, "If we say that we have no sin, we are deceiving ourselves, and the truth is not in us. If we confess our sins, He is faithful and righteous to forgive us our sins" (1:8-9).

## Good Works Do Not Save

The fifth section is a denial that our good works are meritorious. Though they are truly good, because they are the result of God's working in us; yet, as our actions, they are imperfect and defiled. There is an echo here of the chapter on justification, and of the passages that teach our salvation is entirely of God's grace, because of the righteousness and death of Christ, and not at all from our works (Eph. 2:8-9).

## Encouragement in Good Works

The sixth section has a word of encouragement for us. Though our obedience will always fall short, yet it is acceptable to God and pleasing to Him, because all its imperfection is covered by the work of Christ. We are to believe the words of the benediction, that God will "equip you in every good thing to do His will, working in you that which is well-pleasing in His sight, through Jesus Christ" (Heb. 13:20-21). God is so gracious that He even rewards us for that which He has enabled us to do. As A. A. Hodge wrote in his commentary on the *Confession*, "The same covenant of grace provides at once for the infusion of grace in the heart, the exercise of grace in the life, and the reward of the grace so exercised. It is all of grace—a grace called reward added to a grace called work" (p. 228).

## Good Works from the Heart

The last section of the chapter addresses the question of "good works" seen in unbelievers. Sometimes we Christians are put to shame by what we observe in the lives of those who do not name the name of Christ. Yet such "goodness" cannot earn God's favor, for the Scripture teaches that to be truly good, an action must not only be something God's Word commands, but must be done for the right motives and in the right way. This may help us in evaluating the behavior of unbelievers, but it should also lead us to self-examination. Are we not often content with outward conformity to the Law, without attending to the condition of our hearts? When we reflect on our own failures in this regard, we will be led to flee again to Christ for cleansing, and to seek earnestly the working of His Spirit in our lives, that we may love and serve Him from the heart.

# 17

## The Perseverance of the Saints

The preceding chapters in the *Confession* have set forth in a beautiful way the benefits of our salvation through Christ. Called to faith and repentance by the Spirit, we have received a new nature, have been justified before God, adopted as His children, and are in the process of being sanctified, to be conformed to the image of Christ. It is a wonderful thing to be a Christian, to enjoy fellowship with God, to know that one's sins are forgiven, to have peace of conscience.

But what of the future? We see in Scripture, and in our own experience, that some of those who once seemed to have a close walk with the Lord have turned away from Him and no longer live as Christians. Is it possible that what happened to them might also happen to us?

This is not an abstract theological question, but a deeply experiential one. The Apostle Paul faced it, as he named some who had fallen away from their profession, such as Hymenaeus and Philetus, "who have strayed concerning the truth…and overthrow the faith of some." Paul's response is twofold: "Nevertheless the solid foundation of God stands, having this seal: 'The Lord knows those who are His,' and 'Let everyone who names the name of Christ depart from iniquity" (2 Tim. 2:17-19).

The answer involves both God's sovereignty and our responsibility. We cannot know the genuineness of another's profession of faith; there will be some who once professed to be believers who, on the day of judgment, will hear the Lord say, "I never knew you" (Matt. 7:23). Though they professed Christ as Lord, they were never truly saved. On the other hand, Christ, the good Shepherd, says, "My sheep hear My voice, and I know them, and they follow Me. And I give them eternal life, and they shall never perish; neither shall anyone snatch them out of My hand" (John 10:27-28).

The second part of Paul's answer stresses our responsibility: We are to depart from sin. Perseverance is God's work, but it does not take place without our involvement. By the grace of God, we continue in faith, repentance, and good works.

This balance between God's sovereignty and human responsibility is clearly expressed in the present chapter of the *Confession*.

## Believers Can Never Completely Fall Away

What perseverance means is expressed in the first section: True believers can never totally or finally fall away from the state of grace. As the third section of the chapter indicates, Christians can partially and temporarily fall into sin. But, if they are truly saved, that is, accepted in Christ, and called and sanctified by the Holy Spirit, they will in the end persevere and be eternally saved. Previous chapters of the *Confession* have explained what it is to be a true believer in Christ. The promise of perseverance in grace belongs only to such.

## God's Will and Work

The basis for perseverance is presented in the second paragraph. First, it does not depend on a person's free will. In chapter 9, the *Confession* points out that in this life the believer, though renewed by the Spirit, "doth not perfectly, nor only, will that which is good, but doth also will that which is evil. The will of man is made perfectly and immutably free to good alone, in the state of glory only" (sections 4-5). Perseverance does not finally rest on our own strength or determination.

Positively, the *Confession* teaches that perseverance rests on God's will and work:

* It rests on the unchangeable decree of election: "He chose us in [Christ] before the foundation of the world, that we should be holy and without blame before Him in love" (Eph. 1:4).
* It rests on the work of Christ, who purchased our eternal salvation by His perfect obedience and sacrificial death (Heb. 9:11-15). Christ not only died, but rose again and now continues to make intercession for us. We learn in John 17 how He prays for us: "Holy Father, keep through Your name those You have given Me. . . . I do not pray that You should take them out of the world, but that you should keep them from the evil one" (vv. 11, 15). We may be certain that the Father hears and answers the prayers of His Son for us.
* Perseverance rests in the continuing presence and work of the Holy Spirit in us. John calls the presence of the Spirit the "anointing," and he writes, "But the anointing you have received from Him abides in you, and . . . teaches you concerning all things, and is true, and is not a lie, and just as it has taught you, you will abide in Him" (1 John 2:27).
* Perseverance rests on the "seed" of God remaining in us. This expression is taken from 1 John 3:9, where it is connected with the new birth. A. A. Hodge explains that it means "the new spiritual principles and tendencies implanted in regeneration."
* Finally, perseverance rests on the nature of the covenant of grace. One striking passage cited by the *Confession* in reference to the covenant is Jeremiah 32:40: "And I will make an everlasting covenant with them, that I will not turn away from doing them good; but I will put My fear in their hearts so that they will not depart from Me."

Perseverance in grace is thus seen to be truly of grace; it is a part of the whole package of the gracious salvation God has provided for His people through Christ. We also note that perseverance rests on a trinitarian basis: election by the Father, atonement and intercession by the Son, and renewal and sanctification by the Holy Spirit.

## Human Responsibility

The third section of the chapter deals more particularly with human responsibility and with the reality of Christian experience. The biblical record tells us of many of God's people who stumbled: Noah was guilty of drunkenness, David of adultery and murder, Peter of denying his Lord. The Psalms contain many expressions of doubt and fear, even of anger against the Lord (e.g., "You have renounced the covenant of Your servant," Ps. 89:39).

These partial and temporary failures do not negate the doctrine of perseverance, but they are very serious indeed. They come about because of the continuing strength of temptation by the familiar triad of the world, the flesh, and the devil (here presented in a different order), and by "the neglect of the means of their preservation." Here we are reminded of Jesus' word to His disciples: "Watch and pray, lest you enter into temptation" (Matt. 26:41). The psalmist declared, "Your word have I hidden in my heart, that I might not sin against You" (Ps. 119:11). Neglect of the means of grace leads to backsliding.

The *Confession*, in affirming the certainty of the believer's ultimate victory, does not underestimate the damage done by falling into sin, even temporarily. It results in God's displeasure, grieves the Spirit, takes away our enjoyment of fellowship with God, and harms others. In *The Westminster Confession for the Church Today*, Rowland Ward cites a pertinent comment: "When Satan whispers: 'If you sin, you can repent,' one may respond in Samuel Waldron's words: 'Yes, and you will, but to truly repent is to vomit up the sin. All the enjoyment of eating the dainty morsel is more than made up for by the miserable nausea and vomiting. There will always be more misery than pleasure in sin for a true Christian' " (p. 120).

This chapter of the *Confession* expresses well the confidence regarding the future that Christians possess in Christ. We may well echo Peter's doxology: "Blessed be the God and Father of our Lord Jesus Christ, who according to His abundant mercy has begotten us again to a living hope through the resurrection of Jesus Christ from the dead, to an inheritance incorruptible and undefiled and that does not fade away, reserved in heaven for you, who are kept by the power of God through faith for salvation ready to be revealed in the last time" (1 Pet. 1:3-5). ⊕

# 18

# Assurance

This chapter brings to a close the *Westminster Confession of Faith*'s teaching about the way of salvation, which began with chapter 7, "Of God's Covenant with Man." Thus, no less than 12 of the *Confession*'s 33 chapters are concerned directly with the gospel of Christ.

This chapter on assurance addresses profound personal and practical questions: "Can I be sure that my sins are forgiven?" "Can I know that I have been accepted by God?" "Can I be confident that after this life I will live forever?"

Before the Reformation, the Catholic Church had taught that it was evidence of pride and presumption for anyone to claim assurance of salvation (apart from a special revelation given to a very few). Then came the rediscovery of the gospel of free grace, as Luther and other Reformers learned from the Bible that Jesus Christ had done everything necessary for our salvation by His obedient life and sacrificial death.

Forgiveness of sins and eternal life are given freely by God to those who acknowledge their sin and trust in Jesus for salvation. When it is understood that salvation rests entirely on what Christ has done, and not at all on our own performance, then humble assurance of salvation becomes possible. The Apostle John writes, "These things I have written to you who believe in the name of the Son of God, that you may know that you have eternal life" (1 John 5:13). The teachings of 1 John are faithfully reflected in this chapter.

## Warning

The chapter begins with a note of warning, which is needed in our day. There is a danger of false assurance. "Hypocrites, and other unregenerate men, may vainly deceive themselves with false hopes, and carnal presumptions of being in the favour of God, and estate of salvation." In America, polls indicate that as much as 40 percent of the population regard themselves as "born again," and yet many of those people seem to show no evidence of living the Christian life. Jesus warned of those who called Him "Lord, Lord" and yet did not do the things He said. At the Judgment Day, He will declare to them, "I never knew you; depart from me, you who practice lawlessness!" (Matt. 7:21-23)

Only the Holy Spirit can give us a genuine assurance of salvation. We should be careful in evangelism not to demand of those who have just received Christ that they immediately affirm that they are sure of their salvation. The Spirit may give that to some; but the teaching of this chapter is that full assurance is ordinarily the product of a process of growth and reflection that may take some time.

## A Valid Claim

After its warning, the first section indicates the kind of person who may validly claim assurance: "such as truly believe in the Lord Jesus, and love Him in sincerity, endeavouring to walk in all good conscience before Him." That is, assurance is for those who are real Christians, born again by the Spirit of God.

## Peace With God

The second section of the chapter speaks of the assurance available to true believers as "infallible," rather than "conjectural" or "probable." The language here seems to be taken from the earlier Puritan writer William Perkins, who also spoke of assurance as "undoubting." It seems that "infallible" is not used in an absolute sense. Section 4 asserts that true believers do not always enjoy total assurance. "Infallible assurance" seems to be used to describe the experience of one who is not constantly paralyzed by doubt and uncertainty, but who lives, at least most of the time, with a strong sense of being at peace with God because of what Christ has done.

It is the experience described by Paul in these words: "For I know whom I have believed, and am persuaded that He is able to keep what I have committed to Him until that day" (2 Tim. 1:12).

This strong assurance rests on a foundation that has three elements.

- The first element is "the divine truth of the promises of salvation." When tempted to doubt, we are to flee to the promises of God in His Word, and to Jesus Christ, in whom all those promises are Yes and Amen (2 Cor. 1:20). I remember a time of spiritual struggle in my youth, when I found great help in reading aloud the petitions and the promises of Psalm 119. Assurance comes by believing the infallible truth of the Word of God, as it shows Christ to us in all His grace and saving power.

- The second element of the foundation of assurance is "the inward evidence of those graces unto which these promises are made." In one sense, the promises of salvation are conditional. God does not promise that everyone without exception will be saved. He promises salvation to those who are contrite, to those who repent of their sin, to those who receive His Son, to those who call upon His name. So we must examine ourselves to see if there is evidence that we have met those conditions: "Do I sorrow for my sin?", "Have I repented?", and so on. It is important in such self-examination, however, that we look for the reality of our faith, and not its strength or perfection.

To keep us from the error of thinking that these inward qualities are our own doing, the product of self-effort, the *Confession* calls them "graces." In order to receive God's salvation, we must repent and believe. The Scripture makes clear, however, that our ability to do these things is the gift of God's grace (Eph. 2:8-9; Acts 11:18).

The third element in the basis for assurance is "the testimony of the Spirit of adoption witnessing with our spirits that we are the children of God." There was a difference of opinion among the members of the Westminster Assembly as to the way in which this witness of the Spirit is experienced. Some believed that the Spirit gives assurance by enabling believers to discern the graces wrought by the Spirit in their lives. Others held that the Spirit works directly in the heart to give assurance, without the use of evidences. The language here was apparently adopted in order to accommodate both views. It is clear, however, that all three elements are important. We must look not only within ourselves, but also to Christ and His Word, if we are to have true assurance. And assurance is ultimately the gift of the Holy Spirit, who always works by and with the Word.

## The End of a Process

The third section speaks of assurance coming at the end of a process for many. It is not automatically given when one first believes. It should be sought; however, one is not to seek some extraordinary experience to be sure of his or her salvation. Assurance normally comes by the means of grace: reading the Word, listening to preaching, praying, observing the sacraments, participating in fellowship. Remember Answer 172 of the *Westminster Larger Catechism*: "One who doubteth of his being in Christ...may have true interest in Christ, though he be not yet assured thereof; and in God's account hath it, if he be duly affected with the apprehension of the want of it, and unfeignedly desires to be found in Christ, and to depart from iniquity: in which case [because promises are made, and this Sacrament is appointed, for the relief even of weak and doubting Christians]...he may and ought to come to the Lord's Supper, that he may be further strengthened."

This section also speaks of the results of assurance: peace, joy, love, thankfulness, strength, and cheerfulness. So desirable are these lovely fruits, that there need be no fear that assurance will result in a careless and wicked life, as some have charged.

## Loss of Assurance

The final section deals with what may be called the interruption of assurance. It parallels the final section of the chapter on perseverance, in allowing for the ups and downs of Christian experience. For His own good reasons, God sometimes permits His children to lose their assurance. Such a loss, however, does not mean that they have lost their salvation, and the Holy Spirit is able to renew the blessed assurance of salvation in His own time and way.

Many of the Psalms give us appropriate words to use in such times. Think of Psalm 73: "But as for me, my feet had almost stumbled; my feet had nearly slipped. For I was envious of the boastful, when I saw the prosperity of the wicked.... Nevertheless, I am continually with you; you hold me by my right hand. You will guide me with your counsel, and afterward receive me to glory" (vv. 2-3, 23-24).

# 19

# The Law of God

When we sing Psalm 119 (and also other psalms) we express our love for and delight in God's law, and our intention and desire to live in obedience to it. The present chapter of the *Confession* embodies the perspective of Psalm 119, and gives the scriptural basis for this deep appreciation for the law of God. It guides us safely between the errors of legalism (seeking to win acceptance with God by keeping the law) and antinominianism (living as we please without seeking to follow God's law).

## "Written on Their Hearts"

The first section of the chapter discusses the law as a covenant of works. (This is a larger echo of what has already been discussed in chapter 7, section 2.) How was the law given to Adam? We have no record of God giving to him the Ten Commandments. However, Colossians 3:10 implies that being created in the image of God meant having knowledge of the truth. Since even sinful people today show "the work of the law written on their hearts" (Rom. 2:14-15), it is clear that Adam originally knew well the principles of God's law. Sin obscured that knowledge but did not obliterate it entirely.

God continues to deal with all people in terms of the law as a covenant of works. This explains the otherwise puzzling passage in Romans 2:5-10, where Paul seems to teach salvation by works: God "will render to each one according to his deeds." Seen covenantally, Paul's words are preparing for the presentation of the gospel that begins in chapter 3. He is showing us our sinfulness, and the judgment to which we are liable, in order that we may flee to Christ for salvation. All the elements of the covenant of works are in that passage: the command of full obedience, the promise of life, and the threat of death.

## The Rule for Human Life

Since the Fall, no one can be saved by the covenant of works, but the Law of God continues to be the rule for human life. As section 2 states, God continued to make His will known, especially in the giving of the Ten Commandments to Moses. The *Confession* repeats the common understanding of the "two tables" on which God wrote the law: The first table, or tablet, contained commands 1-4, pertaining to our duty to God, the second table commands 5-10, pertaining to our duty to our neighbors. Recent study of ancient covenant documents suggests that the two tables were in fact duplicate copies of the entire law.

In the end, the difference of understanding is not significant, because Jesus teaches us that the law can be summarized in love for God and love for our neighbor (Matt. 22:37-40). The Decalogue is a summary of the law of God. This does not mean that every duty God requires of us can be directly derived from one or other of the commandments, but that, as A. A. Hodge wrote in *The Confession of Faith*: "Every specific duty taught in any portion of Scripture may more or less directly be referred to one or other of the general precepts taught in the Decalogue" (p. 252).

## Ceremonial and Judicial Law

Sections 3 and 4 discuss two other kinds of law found in the Old Testament: the ceremonial and the judicial. The *Confession* here is repeating an ancient distinction within the laws of the Bible, which is found in the writings of Thomas Aquinas, Philip Melanchthon, and John Calvin. Unlike the Ten Commandments (summarizing the moral law), these kinds of law are not permanently binding on all people everywhere. The ceremonial law was for Israel as a church in its infancy, governing her worship and life, pointing forward to the person and saving work of Christ. As Galatians and Hebrews make clear, these regulations were temporary and are no longer applicable as binding law to the people of God.

The judicial laws were for Israel as a nation, and, except for principles of "general equity," are no longer binding, since the nation of Israel no longer exists as a political entity. This is a much-disputed section in the *Confession* since the rise of the so-called "Theonomy" movement.

Realizing the complexity of the issues, the Assembly's meaning in this section seems to be in conformity with Calvin's view as expressed in his *Institutes*, Book IV, Chapter XX. In the 14th section, he discusses "Old Testament law and the laws of nations." He warns of those who "dangerously go astray" by insisting that a properly constituted commonwealth must conform its laws to the political system of Moses. In his view, "the form of their judicial laws, although it had no other intent than how best to preserve that very love which is enjoined by God's eternal law, had something distinct from that precept of love…when these judicial laws were taken away, the perpetual duties and precepts of love could still remain."

Calvin taught that nations had considerable freedom in making their laws, providing they embodied the principles of the permanent moral law of God, which were found not only in the Ten Commandments, but also in "natural law." For example, no nation ought to have laws that honor thieves or permit promiscuous sexual intercourse. In the matter of punishments, he thought that nations had to adjust to circumstances, adopting milder or more severe punishments depending on the state of society.

Calvin's views are not the final authority, of course. But the general strong agreement of the Westminster Assembly with Calvin's positions suggest that in this section they are substantially guided by his writings.

## Conforming to God's Will

Section 5 repeats the truth that the moral law is permanently binding on all people, both because of its content, which reflects the nature and will of the Creator, and because God continues to require of all conformity to His revealed will.

## The Law's Usefulness

Section 6, the longest of the chapter, deals with the usefulness of the moral law to believers in Christ. It stands in sharp contrast to much teaching in professedly Christian circles about not being "under law, but under grace." The section makes a number of points. First, we are not under the law in the sense that we can be either justified or condemned by our performance in relation to it. When we are justified by faith in Christ, we can never come again into condemnation (John 5:24; Rom. 8:1).

Then the *Confession* states a number of ways in which the law is useful to Christians:

⊛ It serves as our rule of life, directing us as to how we may live to please God. The *Larger Catechism* (Q. 97) agrees with the *Heidelberg Catechism* in pointing out that our motive for this obedience is gratitude. The law shows us how to express our thankfulness to God for His great mercy in saving us.

⊛ The law keeps us humble, by continuing to make us aware of the ways in which we fall short of the glory of God. In this way we keep being pointed to Christ, that we may flee to Him as our only refuge.

- The law discourages us from following the tendencies to sin that remain in us. Here the warnings of the law are a help: "The threatenings of it serve to show what even their sins deserve, and what afflictions in this life they may expect for them." Though our eternal salvation is secure when we trust in Christ, it remains true even for the Christian that "the way of the transgressor is hard." God loves us too much to let us go on in disobedience, and if necessary He will chasten us in order to bring us back to the right path (Heb. 12:3-11).
- On the other hand, the promises attached to God's law encourage us in the path of obedience: "The promises of it...shew God's approbation of obedience, and what blessings they may expect [note, not what they deserve] upon the performance thereof."

This perspective on the law, with its warnings and promises, sheds light on the covenantal passages of the New Testament; for example, the quotation from Psalm 34 in 1 Peter 3:8-12. The path of obedience is ever the path of blessing for God's people.

## The Harmony of Law and Grace

To make it clear that law is not the enemy of grace, the chapter concludes with a brief statement of the harmony between them. For the Christian, obedience to the law is not undertaken grudgingly, nor in his or her own strength. Obedience is the product of the work of the Holy Spirit in our lives, making us both willing and able to do God's will.

In this life, that obedience is imperfect, but it is real. Obedience is the fruit of grace, and it brings pleasure to God, and blessing to the believer.

In the light of the truth here presented, we may well sing, "Make me to follow Thy commands, for they my joy maintain. Thy testimonies claim my heart. Keep me from love of gain" (Ps. 119:35-36).

# 20

# Christian Liberty, and Liberty of Conscience

This chapter has a double title, because it deals with two related, but clearly distinct subjects. It is unfortunate that the two are often confused. "Christian liberty" is about matters which are at the heart of the gospel of grace. "Liberty of conscience" is about the relation between the individual's convictions and human authority, both civil and ecclesiastical.

## Liberty in Christ

The first section of the chapter is about the liberty we have in Christ. In writing to the Galatian church, which was in danger of following "another gospel," Paul wrote, "Stand fast therefore in the liberty by which Christ has made us free, and do not be entangled again with a yoke of bondage" (Gal. 5:1). The *Confession* rightly emphasizes that our freedom is due to Christ; He purchased it for us. One of the words for salvation is "redemption," and redemption means "deliverance by the payment of a price." By nature, we are in bondage to sin, self, the powers of evil, and the judgment of God. When we trust in Christ, we are set free. Jesus said,

"If you abide in My word, you are My disciples indeed. And you shall know the truth, and the truth shall make you free. Therefore, if the Son makes you free, you shall be free indeed" (John 8:31-32, 36).

No less than eleven aspects of our freedom in Christ are mentioned. The phrases of the *Confession*'s statement are drawn more or less directly from the proof texts that are given, and it is not easy to determine why they are given in the order that they are. Some of them are related to justification: freedom from the guilt of sin, the wrath of God, the curse of the moral law and everlasting damnation. Also related to justification is the positive blessing of having free access to God. Other phrases relate to sanctification: freedom from the evil world, from bondage to Satan, and from the dominion of sin. (Note the familiar triad: the world, the flesh, and the devil.) Positively, we are set free in Christ to serve God, not as slaves, but as His dear children.

### Old Testament versus New Testament

When this section uses the phrases "under the law" and "under the gospel" it is speaking of the time of the Old Testament and time of the New Testament. The Church is one in all ages, so that, as the *Confession* says, all the blessings which have been described "were common also to believers under the law." But there are also differences between the Old Testament and the New Testament. Now, believers are no longer under the ceremonial law: There is no longer a special priesthood, for Christ is our priest. There are no more animal sacrifices, because Christ by the one great sacrifice of Himself on the cross has fully provided for our salvation (Heb. 10:12-14). Dietary laws and other regulations, which emphasized Israel's separation from other nations, no longer apply, because now Jew and Gentile come together on the same basis in the Church (Eph. 2:11-22). Another difference is a matter of degree: Because of the finished work of Christ, New Testament believers enjoy "greater boldness of access to the throne of grace." In the Temple, worshipers could not enter into the place of God's presence, but were only represented there by the priests. Now that Christ has come, the veil is removed, and we are encouraged to "come boldly to the throne of grace" (Heb. 4:16). We also enjoy "fuller communications of the free Spirit of God." "Communication" is used here in the sense of "imparting" and means that we enjoy a greater measure of the Spirit's teaching, gifts, and power than did Old Testament saints (Acts 2:16-18). The phrase "free Spirit" is evidently taken from Psalm 51:12 in the King James Version. The Assembly no doubt meant by this phrase that the Holy Spirit is generous and bountiful, as He imparts His gifts to us.

## Liberty of Conscience

The remaining sections of the chapter are devoted to the subject of liberty of conscience. This was a pressing issue for the members of the Westminster Assembly. They were Puritans, who had been persecuted in the church and nation for refusing to observe ceremonies prescribed by the bishops under the direction of Charles I. The bishops were requiring such things as turning the communion table into an altar, kneeling to receive communion, wearing ecclesiastical vestments, and making the sign of the cross in baptism. Because these were not warranted in Scripture, many Puritan ministers refused to perform them and suffered severe penalties for their refusal. (See George Gillespie's "A Dispute Against the English Popish Ceremonies.")

By "conscience" the *Confession* means an inward conviction about what God requires. Violation of this inward conviction would result in fearing God's displeasure, and seeking His forgiveness. Liberty of conscience is an application of the principle of the first chapter of the *Confession*—that we learn what we are to believe and what God requires of us from the Scripture alone. If any human authority, civil or ecclesiastical, commands us to believe or do something that is contrary to God's Word, we know immediately that this is not something God requires, and our conscience is therefore free.

### Conscience in Faith and Worship

There is another, more restricted sphere in which the conscience is free: "matters of faith and worship." In this sphere, nothing may be imposed on the conscience which is "beside" the Word. Here the *Confession* states the "regulative principle." God's people may not be required to believe anything not taught in Scripture, and they may not be required to follow any practice in the worship of God which is not warranted by Scripture. To follow mere human authority in these matters is a betrayal of liberty of conscience. Human authorities which attempt to impose extra-biblical beliefs or worship practices are destroying liberty of conscience. They are doing what the scribes did in Jesus' day: "And in vain they worship Me, teaching as doctrines the commandments of men" (Matt. 15:9).

Freedom is precious. Freedom is also liable to be abused. Paul wrote to the Galatians, "For you, brethren, have been called to liberty; only do not use liberty as an opportunity for the flesh, but through love serve one another" (Gal. 5:13). The *Confession* follows Paul in devoting two sections to warnings against those who sin, upon pretense of Christian liberty. Section three quotes from Luke 1:74-75 to emphasize the end or purpose of Christian liberty, which is a life of godliness.

### Preventing Abuse of Christian Liberty

The fourth section sets forth the proper function of human authority in preventing abuses arising from the pretense of Christian liberty. The sentence structure of this section is very complicated; to understand it clearly, we need to break it down into several assertions.

- Human authority ordained by God is not the enemy of Christian liberty. The two are intended to complement one another.
- Human authority cannot deal with inner conviction, that is, with the conscience; that is known to God alone. Human authority is limited to dealing with "published opinions" and "practices"—things which are public knowledge. This rules out anything like the Spanish

Inquisition, which tortured people to extract from them confessions of their inward beliefs.

- ✸ Offenses which are subject to censure by human authority are those contrary to "the light of nature, the known principles of Christianity or the power of godliness." The "light of nature" means general revelation; even the Gentiles, says Paul, have the work of the law written in their hearts (Rom. 2:14-15). "Known principles of Christianity" refers to that which the Church has acknowledged as true through the ages, as expressed in her creeds and confessions based upon Scripture. It is not clear what is meant by "the power of godliness," in distinction from the first two standards. However, the practical concern of the Assembly comes to expression here. Any teaching or example which encourages immoral behavior might be censured by the authorities of church and state.

- ✸ One other kind of offense that is censurable by human authority is teaching or behavior which "are destructive to the external peace and order which Christ has established in the church." In the exercise of their liberty, conscientious people need to be careful that they do not become sinfully disruptive and divisive. Paul's warning to the partisans in the Corinthian church was: "If anyone defiles the temple of God, God will destroy him. For the temple of God is holy, which temple you are" (1 Cor. 3:17).

We cannot deal here with the complicated issue of the proper role of the civil magistrate in relation to the church, and in matters of faith and practice. That subject will come up again for discussion in connection with chapters 23, 30, and 31.

Many people think that the Christian life is narrow, cramped, restricted. The Bible's picture of life with God is far different. Without Christ, we are truly in bondage. When we commit our lives to Him, He sets us free, giving us what Paul calls "the glorious liberty of the children of God" (Rom. 8:21). But that liberty has limits; properly used, it will lead to a life of godliness within the fellowship of the Church.   ⊕

# 21

# Worship and the Sabbath Day

From one perspective, the Westminster Assembly would not have met had it not been for the issue of the public worship of the church. The attempt of Charles I to impose new liturgy on the Church of Scotland in 1637 provoked a widespread resistance, which led to the National Covenant of 1638 and the reestablishment of Presbyterianism in Scotland. The Bishops' Wars of 1639 and 1640 drained the English treasury and forced the king to call the Parliament in order to raise taxes. That "Long" Parliament, led by Puritans, called the Westminster Assembly to advise it in the further reformation of the doctrine, worship, and government of the Church of England.

The Assembly expressed its advice regarding worship in *The Directory for the Publick Worship of God*, and included this chapter in the *Confession of Faith* to set forth the doctrine that should govern the worship of God's people.

## Why We Worship

The chapter begins by stating the reason for worship: the existence, lordship, sovereignty, and goodness of God.

Echoing Romans 1, the *Confession* states that these are known by "the light of nature," that is, by general or natural revelation. The inclusion of the "goodness" of God, as seen in nature, follows Calvin's emphasis on this point. (See the *Institutes*, Book I, Chap. V.) God has planted the "seed of religion" in all people, and so all people worship. Since the Fall, however, they worship created things instead of the Creator (Rom. 1:18-25).

The chapter does not give a definition of worship, but describes it by using active verbs: God is to be "feared, loved, praised, called upon, trusted in, and served" with one's whole being. Stress is placed here on the fact that worship comes from the heart and is not primarily an outward performance. The emphasis on worship from the heart is continued in later sections, when the specific activities of worship are discussed.

The first section also states the basic rule for worship that was central in the Calvinistic Reformation. We call it the regulative principle of worship: "But the acceptable way of worshipping the true God is instituted by himself, and so limited by his own revealed will, that he may not be worshipped according to the imaginations and devices of men…[in any] way not prescribed in the holy Scripture."

Calvin expressed this principle in many places; for example, in commenting on Amos 5:27: "We ought not to bring anything of our own when we worship God, but we ought to depend always on the word of his mouth, and to obey what he has commanded…lest we attempt anything but what he approves" (*Commentary on Amos*, p. 298). This principle is an application of the sufficiency of Scripture, as expressed in the first chapter of the *Confession*. It is also involved in liberty of conscience, as discussed in chapter 20. The principle is based in part on the second commandment and on Jesus' warning in Matthew 15:9.

## Why We Worship God Alone

The second section makes the point that only the triune God is the proper object of worship, and that Christ is the only mediator who can make our worship acceptable to God. Chapters 2 and 8 of the *Confession* give the scriptural and doctrinal basis for this limitation. The adoration and invocation of saints or of any other creature are thus forbidden.

## Prayer

The *Confession* gives prominence to prayer in its discussion of the specific activities of worship. We do not pray acceptably if we attempt to do so in our own righteousness, or in our own strength. Prayer is acceptable when we rely on the mediation and intercession of Christ, and when we depend on the Holy Spirit to guide and enable us as we pray. True prayer is to be from the heart: with "understanding, reverence, humility, fervency, faith, love and perseverance." It will be profitable for the reader to ponder his or her own prayer life in relation to these qualities, and to meditate on the Scripture passages that are listed in the *Confession*. For those who want to go deeper, Calvin's 70-page discussion of prayer in the *Institutes* (Book III, Chap. XX) will reward careful reading.

The proper content of prayer is stated both positively and negatively. We are to pray for things according to God's will (which we learn from the Scripture), and for things lawful, and for all sorts of people. Negatively, we are not to pray for those who have died, or for those who have sinned unto death. In this last point the *Confession* simply repeats 1 John 5:16. Calvin says that the sin unto death is apostasy but warns, since it is rare for us to know that that sin has been committed, "love should dispose us to hope well" regarding those who are living in sin and unbelief (*Commentary on 1 John*, p. 270).

## Elements of Worship

Section 5 sets forth the ordinary elements of public worship: reading of Scripture (having its own importance in worship apart from preaching); preaching and hearing the Word; singing of psalms; administration of the sacraments of baptism and the Lord's supper. To understand in more detail what the Assembly believed about each of these, see the *Directory for Publick Worship*.

The Assembly advocated the exclusive use of the biblical Psalms in praise. With this as the only approved manual for praise, the assembly produced a metrical Psalter containing only the 150 Psalms. The Assembly's Psalter was later revised in Scotland and became the Scottish Psalter of 1650.

Note well the emphasis on the inwardness and spirituality of worship in this section. True worship must not only have the correct activities but must be from the heart. Scripture reading must be "with godly fear," preaching must be "sound," hearing must be "conscionable (conscientious)," singing must be "with grace in the heart," sacraments must be received "in a worthy manner." Correct form and inward devotion go together. Our Covenanter churches have emphasized the continuing observance of the regulative principle of worship. We must also continue to stress, as the Puritans did, that acceptable worship is a matter of the heart.

The elements listed above were ordinary parts of worship. They also listed other, extraordinary worship activities, such as religious oaths and vows (involved in public covenanting), times of fasting and thanksgiving. These were to be observed when appropriate, as determined by the Church's interpretation of God's providential dealings with them.

## Meeting Houses

Section 6 expresses the truth taught by Jesus in John 4:21-24: Because of His accomplishing salvation for His people by His life, death, and resurrection, there are no longer any special holy places where worship is to take place. Churches are "meeting houses" where worship takes place, but they have no special sanctity. The persecuted Covenanters knew that well, as they met in their conventicles on the moors.

## Sabbath Observance

The last two sections of the chapter deal with the observance of the Sabbath. These express the conviction that the fourth commandment has not been repealed. The Sabbath was revealed at the time of creation, was observed before the giving of the Law at Sinai, and was included in the Decalogue, the permanent summary of God's will for mankind. Christ is the Lord of the Sabbath (Mark 2:28). Since His resurrection it is called the Lord's Day (see Rev. 1:10), in remembrance of His victory over sin and death, so that now it is observed on the first day of the week. On this day we not only remember God's great works of creation and redemption, but look forward to the completion of redemption and the renewal of creation in that "Sabbath rest" that awaits the people of God (Heb. 4:9).

The Assembly's high view of the Sabbath is in sharp contrast to the modern carelessness about the day. Perhaps they did not give enough emphasis to the biblical teaching that an important reason for the Sabbath was rest, and, as Nigel Lee has said in his book *The Covenantal Sabbath*, they tended to turn the day into a "religious working day" (p. 260). But we should be challenged by this strong statement of the obligation of Sabbath-keeping to make better use of the day for the nurture of our souls. The Sabbath commandment is a gracious one, intended for our blessing. May we call the Sabbath a delight, as did the Puritans.                    ⊕

# 22

## What are Biblical Oaths and Vows?

The Westminster Assembly included this chapter in the *Confession* not only because the subject of oaths and vows is addressed in the Bible, but also because there were many controversies about this matter in their historical situation. Some Anabaptists, and later the Quakers, refused to take any oaths. The Roman Catholic Church insisted on the legitimacy of the vows of obedience, chastity (celibacy), and poverty taken by the clergy.

Both the Scottish Covenanters and the English Puritans drew up and swore their fidelity to covenants, such as the National Covenant of 1638 and the Solemn League and Covenant of 1643. The word *covenant* does not appear in this chapter, but the practice of "public social covenanting" was in the minds of the Assembly as they wrote this chapter. Some members of the Assembly, and later generations of Covenanters, suffered greatly because of their adherence to the covenants they had solemnly sworn before God.

The first four sections of this chapter are concerned with the subject of oaths, and the last three with the subject of vows. While the similarity between them is acknowledged, the difference lies in the fact that oaths serve to confirm assertions or promises made between men, while vows are promises made to God.

## Oaths

Section 1 describes what is meant by an oath. First, it is an act of religious worship. This does not mean that it is part of every worship service, but that an oath involves invoking God to be witness to what is said or promised. If the Lord's name is not to be taken in vain, the one who swears must acknowledge the living God as one who sees the thoughts and intents of the heart, and who will see to it that truth and justice prevail. Since an oath calls upon God in that way, it is an act of worship.

Second, an oath confirms either an assertion or a promise. In a court of law, for example, the truthfulness of one's testimony is confirmed with an oath. When a person assumes office in the church, or in civil government, he promises fidelity in the future, and calls on God to witness the sincerity of his intention.

### "Lawful Oaths"

The *Confession* defends the taking of oaths, in opposition to the Anabaptist rejection of all swearing. In section 2, the teaching of Jesus in the Sermon on the Mount (Matt. 5:33-37) on the subject of oaths is in view. The *Confession* understands Jesus' main point to be that oaths are not to be taken lightly, but with due reverence for the name of God. The scribes and Pharisees allowed for lesser oaths, invoking other things than the name of God, and then taught that such oaths were not binding. Jesus taught that, ordinarily, one's word should be sufficient, so that the need for oaths is rare. But since earlier in the sermon He made it clear that He did not come to abolish the law of Moses (Matt. 5:17-18), and since that law commanded that oaths be taken on appropriate occasions (Deut. 10:20), Jesus was not here forbidding all oath-taking. He Himself did not refuse to answer when placed on oath before Pilate (Matt. 26:63). So, says the *Confession*, "a lawful oath, being imposed by lawful authority...ought to be taken." Such an oath must be taken only in the name of God. This basic principle is repeated at the end of section 3.

### Proper Content for Oaths

The third section discusses the proper content of an oath. In testifying, one may only invoke God's name to confirm "what he is fully persuaded is the truth." In binding himself to future performance, one may only do so in relation to what is, in his sincere belief, good and just; to what he is able to perform, and to what he is resolved to perform. The oath sworn by Paul's enemies, not to eat or drink until they killed him (Acts 23:12), was a wicked oath. We cannot bind ourselves to do what is displeasing to God, and then think that He holds us responsible to perform our promise. Such oaths are to be repented of, not carried out.

### Oaths Must Be Wholeheartedly Taken

The fourth section has in mind the teaching of some Jesuits of that time, that oaths could be taken with mental reservations, or that they were not binding if required by Protestant authorities. The purpose of oaths is to promote truthfulness, and it is a contradiction to use an oath to cover a deceitful purpose. An oath invokes God's judgment on one who is unfaithful. Such an action is not to be taken lightly. The third commandment warns, "The Lord will not hold him guiltless who takes his name in vain" (Ex. 20:7).

## Vows

Section 5 introduces the subject of vows and stresses the similarity between vows and promissory oaths, especially in regard to obligation.

### Vows versus Oaths

The distinction between an oath and a vow is made in section 6. An oath is made in the name of God to confirm a transaction between men. A vow "is not to be made to any creature, but to God alone." It is a promise given to God regarding future actions or patterns of life. Another distinction is that, whereas an oath may be imposed by lawful authority, a vow is voluntary. This point is made in two important passages on vows, Deuteronomy 23:21-23 and Ecclesiastes 5:4-5. Both teach that one who does not vow does not sin. However, if one does vow, then one is obligated to perform what he has promised.

Although vows are voluntary, they are not to be arbitrary; that is, they are to be made "out of faith, and conscience of duty." This means that we must be governed by the Scriptures in our vows, for otherwise we could not know what is pleasing to God. Vows may strengthen our resolve to live as God requires, or they may commit us to particular actions that will help us to live in obedience. Calvin wrote on this point: "Let us not take to ourselves such license as to dare vow to God that which bears no evidence as to how he may esteem it. For Paul's teaching that whatever is done apart from faith is sin...is applicable" (*Institutes*, Book IV, Chap. XIII:3).

The *Confession* indicates that vows express our thankfulness or are a means to obtain what we desire. Hannah's vow to give her son to the Lord is an example of the latter (1 Sam. 1:11). In the light of previous chapters on justification and good works, however, we should be careful not to think that some special performance will merit God's blessing. Only as vows and their performance result in a closer, more loving relationship with the Lord can we expect that His face will shine more brightly upon us.

## Limitations on Vows

Certain cautions or limitations on taking vows are stated in section 7. Vows cannot bind to what is contrary to God's Word, nor to what would be a hindrance to our obedience to His Word. One must not vow to perform something "which is not within his own power, or for the performance whereof he hath no promise or ability from God."

In other words, vows should not be unrealistic or presumptuous. Here the *Confession* has in view Roman Catholic teaching on vows, as is specifically indicated in the reference to monastic vows at the end of the section. It was the Reformation conviction that such vows were harmful, and that those who had taken them were not bound by them. Former monks and priests, such as Martin Luther, John Calvin, and John Knox, had violated those promises out of loyalty to the gospel.

In conclusion, we make two practical observations. First, in the light of the cautions of this chapter about the serious obligations of oaths and vows, and the dangers of taking them improperly, we may well heed the words of Calvin: "Anyone who obeys my advice will undertake only sober and temporary vows" (*Institutes*, Book IV, Chap. XIII:6).

Second, in light of the description of vows as voluntary, and made to God alone, we may question whether we should regard professions and promises made for church membership, or for holding office in the church, as "vows." It may be more accurate to regard them as made to the church, with God as our witness. This would not diminish their solemnity and obligation, but would make our way of speaking of them more consistent with the language of the *Confession*.

# 23

# The Civil Magistrate

Civil government touches our lives in many ways, for good or ill, and we need to have a biblical perspective on the just authority of civil government, and also on the limitation of that authority. Much of the struggle of our Covenanter forefathers was about the proper relationship of the Christian and the church to the state. That is the subject of chapter 23 of the *Westminster Confession of Faith*.

It should not be surprising that the *Westminster Confession* includes a chapter dealing with civil government. Nearly all of the confessions of the Reformation had similar statements, and Calvin included a chapter on the civil magistrate in his *Institutes*. There is much history and much teaching in the Bible dealing with rulers—Psalm 2 and Romans 13 are examples.

## Government Is Legitimate

Given the imperfection and abuses of government, some Christians are tempted to become virtual anarchists, opposed to all civil authority. Against that temptation, the first section of chapter 23 of the *Confession* affirms the legitimacy of civil authority. "God...hath ordained civil magistrates to be under him over the people, for his own glory and the publick good." Ultimately, the power of civil government comes from God, as Paul wrote in Romans 13:1-7, calling civil magistrates "servants of God." Governments exercise awesome power over the lives and property of their citizens. When that power is exercised in a proper way, to encourage good behavior and punish bad, it is to be respected as coming from God. We are often disappointed in our governments, and sometimes oppressed by them. The biblical teaching, however, is that they derive their just power, not from "the consent of the governed," but from God. Since this is so, rulers are accountable to God for the way they use the authority He has given them.

The *Confession* does not speak explicitly of the duty of the state to acknowledge the authority of Christ and His law, a point that is of great importance in the historical testimony of the Reformed Presbyterian churches. The reason for this appears to be that, in the 17th century, all the nations of Europe were professedly Christian and claimed to be ruling in accordance with the law of God. The Covenanters and Puritans who made up the Westminster Assembly were working to see a more consistent expression of this Christian commitment in their governments.

## Government Is Ordained by God

The second section is a response to views of the Anabaptists (e.g., Mennonites), who believed that government was a kind of necessary evil, and that no Christian ought to hold government office or participate in military service. Since Anabaptists had suffered much at the hands of cruel governments, we may sympathize with their view; however, it fails to do justice to the biblical teaching.

If government is ordained by God, to be His servant, then it follows that Christians may participate in government, provided they are not required to disobey God in doing so. Joseph, Daniel, and Nehemiah served in pagan govern-ments. The *Confession* affirms that "Christians [may] accept and execute the office of a magistrate," and that "they ought especially to maintain piety, justice, and peace" in doing so. The historic Covenanter position of political dissent was not based on a belief that all government was evil, but on objections to particular features in the law that were held to be contrary to the law of God. In such cases, "we ought to obey God rather than men" (Acts 5:29).

In the New Testament, soldiers who believed in Christ were not required to abandon their military service. Fre-quently the nation of Israel was commanded by the Lord to fight against their enemies and to trust the Lord for victory. Paul teaches that God has given to government "the power of the sword" (Rom. 13:4). Participation in military service is lawful, provided the war is just and necessary.

The latter principle calls for careful consideration of the ethical justification for a particular military action before a Christian should participate. The *Confession*'s position is neither that of absolute pacifism nor of militarism. A. A. Hodge comments: "War is an incalculable evil, because of the lives it destroys, the misery it occasions, and the moral degradation it infallibly works on all sides....In order to make a war right in God's sight, it is not only necessary that our enemy should aim to do us a wrong, but also (1) That the wrong he attempts should...threaten the national life; and (2) That war be the only means to avert it" (*The Confession of Faith*, p. 296).

It is interesting to note that all the lay members of the Westminster Assembly were members of the English Parlia-ment, which was then engaged in the great Civil War against the forces of Charles I.

## Government and the Church

The third section of the chapter speaks of the authority of civil government in relation to the church. It begins by stating the limitations of such authority: "The civil magistrate may not assume to himself the administration of the Word and sacraments, or the power of the keys of the kingdom of heaven." The latter was understood by the Assembly to be the power of church discipline. With regard to the central functions of the church, the civil ruler had no legitimate authority. The Covenanters and the Puritans resisted the attempts by the Stuart kings to dictate to the church how she was to worship and what she was to believe and preach, calling such attempts "Erastian."

The rest of the section attributes much power to the magistrate in religious matters. It is the right and duty of the civil government, according to the *Confession*, to attempt to preserve the unity and peace of the church, to see that its confession and teaching are pure and complete, to suppress blasphemy and heresy, and to prevent or reform corruptions and abuses in worship and discipline. This right and duty is to be exercised in part by calling and supervising synods.

The Westminster Assembly was describing its own situation and function. The Assembly had been called by the Parliament, its agenda was set by the Parliament, and its conclusions would only become operative through approval by the Parliament. The Assembly was, in fact, not an ecclesiastical court, but an advisory commission of the Parliament.

Later Presbyterians were not willing to take the Westminster Assembly's special situation as a model for the correct relationship between church and state. When the *Confession* was approved by the Church of Scotland in 1647, it made the following qualification, which also applies to this section: "It is further declared, That the Assembly [of the Church of Scotland] understandeth some parts of the second article of the thirty-one chapter only of kirks not settled." In settled churches, the Assembly declared, ministers and ruling elders are free to assemble without the call or permission of the magistrate.

## Government and Christian Behavior

The fourth section summarizes biblical injunctions to Christians in their behavior toward civil government: We are to pray for magistrates, honor them, pay taxes, and obey and submit to their authority, in so far as that authority is not contrary to the law of God. The latter part of the section rejects certain teachings of the Roman Catholic Church at that time: namely, that Christians need not obey an unbelieving or heretical ruler; that members of the clergy were exempt from civil law; and that the Pope could exercise any legitimate civil power.

Both Northern Ireland and the United States are in times of some uncertainty about the futures of our respective governmental systems. In such a time, it is well to remember that "the Lord reigns," and that we are to "put no confidence in princes" (Ps. 97:1; 146:3). It is also a good time to ponder the teaching of this chapter of the *Confession*, and to pray that God will send revival, and that we may have leaders who will seek "to maintain piety, justice, and peace." ⊕

# 24

# Marriage and Divorce

The institution of marriage is under severe attack in our time. In America, one out of two marriages ends in divorce, and it has become commonplace for couples to live together without being married. There is agitation for legal recognition of "marriages" between persons of the same sex.

This is only a sample of the widespread disregard for God's laws regarding marriage. It is good for us, and particularly for young people, to be reminded of what the Bible teaches about God's plan for marriage, as it is explained in this chapter of the *Westminster Confession of Faith*.

## The Definition of Marriage

The first section defines marriage as a union "between one man and one woman." It is God's will that marriage be monogamous. In many societies, including that of the Old Testament, polygamy has been practiced, but always to the loss and harm of the people involved. While the Lord tolerated polygamy in the Old Testament, He gave many indications that it was not His original intention for marriage. The jealousy evident in the families of Abraham, Jacob, and Elkanah bears witness to the evil that is inherent in such a system.

The New Testament calls us to a higher standard, or, rather, calls us back to the original standard. When asked a question about divorce, Jesus spoke of the institution of marriage in the garden of Eden, quoting, "For this reason a man shall leave his father and mother and be joined to his wife [not 'wives'] and the two [not 'three or more'] shall become one flesh" (Matt. 19:5; see Gen. 2:24-25). When God saw that it was not good for Adam to be alone, but that he needed a suitable helper, God made just *one* woman, Eve, to meet that need (Gen. 2:18-24).

The first instance of polygamy occurred in the ungodly line, in the family of Lamech (Gen. 4:19). In the New Testament church, one of the qualifications for an officer was that he should be "husband of one wife" (1 Tim. 3:2, 12). Thus the whole church was called to the practice of monogamy.

The Westminster Assembly could hardly have anticipated the problem we face today of so-called "gay marriages." But their statement of biblical truth is nevertheless helpful to us, because the *Confession* states unambiguously that marriage is between a man and a woman. Because the practice of homosexuality is said in Scripture to be sinful (Rom. 1:26-27; 1 Cor. 6:9-10), there can be no doubt that such unions must be rejected.

## The Purposes of Marriage

The second section speaks of the purposes for which God has ordained marriage: (1) for mutual help of husband and wife; (2) for having children; and (3) for the preventing of "uncleanness" (i.e., sexual immorality). The first two are drawn from the institution of marriage in Genesis 1 and 2; the third from Paul's teaching in 1 Corinthians 7:2.

All the members of the assembly were familiar with the marriage ceremony found in the Anglican *Book of Common Prayer*, which also spoke of the reasons for marriage: "One was, the procreation of children to be brought up in the fear and nurture of the Lord, and praise of God. Secondly, it was ordained for a remedy against sin, and to avoid fornication.... Thirdly, for the mutual society, help, and comfort, that the one ought to have of the other."

The resemblance between the two statements is obvious, but the Assembly has changed the order. We should not make too much of the change of order, but placing "mutual comfort" first gives expression to the positive view the Puritans held of marriage. Instead of being a kind of necessary evil—to produce children and prevent immorality—marriage is first of all for the companionship and enjoyment of the partners. In a day when marriage is disparaged as "only a piece of paper," Christian people ought to exalt the beauty of a permanent, committed relationship that will endure through good and bad times, and that will provide a secure and loving environment in which children can grow up.

## Who Can Marry

The third and fourth sections deal with the persons who can legitimately marry. Marriage is not limited to believers but is a divine ordinance for the whole human race. We know this because it began with the first parents of the human race, and, since the Fall, God holds all people accountable for following His laws about marriage (Heb. 13:4; Luke 3:19-20).

There are some special directions for believers in Christ however. They are "to marry only in the Lord." Throughout the Bible there are warnings against mixed marriages between believers and unbelievers (Deut. 7:2-3; 2 Cor. 6:14). The marriage relationship is intended to be a union of heart and soul as well as body, and if the partners are not agreed in their faith there will be a barrier to full intimacy. The believing partner will frequently have to choose between loyalty to Christ and loyalty to the spouse, and will face strong temptation to compromise. It is for our good that the Lord gives this restriction.

There is also a restriction regarding relatives: "Marriage ought not to be within the degrees of consanguinity and affinity forbidden in the word." "Consanguinity" refers to blood relations, and "affinity" to the corresponding relationships among in-laws. The *Confession* refers to Leviticus 18 and 20 as the source of this restriction.

With regard to the latter, Presbyterians have not been agreed. Most American Presbyterians have modified the *Confession* at this point, though such respected theologians as John Murray and G. I. Williamson have argued that the *Confession* is correct. The statement in the Irish RP *Testimony* (1966) is representative: "Also regarding Chapter XXIV, Paragraph IV, in the matter of marriage with a deceased wife's sister and deceased husband's brother—in view of the uncertainty amongst students of Scripture as to the true interpretation of the injunctions laid down, no disciplinary action is taken by the Church against those who contract such marriages or ministers who perform them."

## Divorce

The last two sections deal with the subject of divorce. Two grounds for lawful divorce are recognized: adultery and desertion. The former is based on the instruction of our Lord in Matthew 19:9. Where a marriage is dissolved because of adultery, the *Confession* specifically says that the "innocent party" is free to remarry.

In the matter of desertion, the Assembly relied on the teaching of Paul in 1 Corinthians 7:15. There the specific case described is that of a marriage where one partner has become a Christian, and the other does not want to continue the marriage. In such cases "a brother or sister is not under bondage," i.e., is free to remarry. The Assembly extends Paul's instruction to other similar cases where one partner is unwilling to continue the marriage.

The emphasis in these sections is not to make divorce easy, but to stress the permanence of marriage. Couples are to be encouraged to work through problems, with divorce being only a last resort, and even then it is limited to two specific grounds. If divorce occurs, it is to be in an orderly and public manner, under the proper authority.

Sometimes the view that sexual behavior is inherently sinful is called the "puritannical view." This is a gross misrepresentation of the value the Puritans placed on marriage and married love. It has been said that the first instance of great literature that placed romantic love within marriage was in the writings of the Puritan John Milton. Following the Bible, the Puritans indeed condemned improper, selfish, and intemperate expressions of sexuality, but they knew well that God created man male and female, and, before the Fall, commanded them to be fruitful and multiply. Sex and marriage are God's good gifts, and, used in a godly way, bring great blessing and enjoyment to God's people.

# 25

# The Church

Modern-day Christians are inclined to think of the
Christian faith in an individualistic way. Our culture,
with its concentration on the self, encourages this trend. We
rightly stress the importance of a personal relationship with
Christ, but this should not result in our underestimating the
importance of the church in helping us to come to experience that relationship, to grow in grace, and to worship and
serve the Lord. The Christian life, rightly understood, is a
life in community.

The Westminster Assembly therefore gave much attention to the teaching of the Scriptures about the church. That
teaching is expressed in this chapter, "Of the Church," and
also in three other chapters: chapter 26 ("Of the Communion
of Saints"); chapter 30 ("Of Church Censures"); and chapter
31 ("Of Synods and Councils"). Even these four chapters do
not contain all that the Assembly wrote on the doctrine of
the church. Before the *Confession* was written, the "Form
of Presbyterian Church-Government" was issued, which
dealt with the subjects of church membership, the officers

of the church, and ordination. The *Confession*'s emphasis on the church will give us a helpful counterbalance to the individualism of our day.

## The Church Visible and Invisible

The first two sections of the chapter deal with the important distinction between the church as invisible, on the one hand, and the church as visible, on the other. These are not two different churches, but rather two ways of looking at the one church of Jesus Christ. The invisible church is the church as known to God alone, which cannot be seen in its full extent by human eyes. The visible church is the church as seen by us, made up of those who profess faith in Christ and join together in worship and service.

Calvin spoke of this distinction in the following words: "Holy Scripture speaks of the church in two ways. Sometimes by the term 'church' it means that which is actually in God's presence, into which no persons are received but those who are children of God by grace of adoption and true members of Christ by sanctification of the Spirit. Then, indeed, the church includes not only the saints presently living on earth, but all the elect from the beginning of the world. Often, however, the name 'church' designates the whole multitude of men spread over the earth who profess to worship one God and Christ" (*Institutes*, IV:1:7).

When Calvin and the *Confession* speak of the invisible church, they have in mind the church as it is described in the first chapter of Ephesians. In the purpose of God, which will surely be accomplished, the church embraces people from all times and places who are chosen, adopted, and redeemed by the blood of Christ, destined to be holy and without blame in the sight of God, enjoying His glorious inheritance.

In contrast to the ultimate perfection of the invisible church, the visible church is imperfect, since it includes some whose profession is only outward. Jesus spoke of the visible church when He gave the parable of the sower, and of the wheat and the tares (Matt. 13).

In both of these sections, the church is spoken of as catholic, or universal. This is a reference to the fact that the church, since the coming of Christ, includes people from all the nations of the world. We have a natural tendency to limit our view of the church in terms of our own ethnic and denominational group (the two often go together). In Christ, however, "there is no Greek or Jew, circumcised or uncircumcised, barbarian, Scythian, slave or free, but Christ is all, and is in all" (Col. 3:11). Viewing the church in this way should encourage us to pray for the work of Christ all over the world, and to sense our essential unity with all those who love the Lord Jesus. And it should encourage us to seek a more visible unity in the church, as Christ prayed (John 17:21).

The Scripture uses rich metaphors to picture the church, which are repeated in these sections: The church is the bride (spouse), body, and kingdom of Christ, the house and family of God. These expressions are explained in the proof texts listed in the *Confession*.

One expression requires a comment. From Ephesians 1:23, the *Confession* applies these words to the church: "the fullness of him that filleth all in all." Some commentators think these words refer to Christ, not the church. Calvin applied them to the church, however, with the following comment: "This is the highest honour of the Church, that, unless He is united to us, the Son of God reckons Himself in some measure imperfect." (For further explanation, consult Calvin's *Commentary on Ephesians*.)

The *Confession* stresses the importance of the visible church by asserting in modified form the claim often made by the Roman Catholic Church: "Out of which [the visible church] there is no ordinary possibility of salvation." This does not mean that church membership saves. It *does* mean that God has established the church to be the instrument of bringing people to salvation, and that normally those who are saved will publicly profess their faith and become active in some congregation of God's people. The word "ordinarily" acknowledges that sometimes God works differently, and that some people are prevented by circumstances from identifying with the church. But it is a rare thing to find a vital, mature, fruitful believer who is not connected to other believers in Christ's church.

## God's Purpose for the Visible Church

The third section of the chapter highlights God's purpose for this visible church: "the gathering and perfecting of the saints"—in other words, evangelism and edification. To accomplish this purpose He has given to the church "ministry, oracles, and ordinances." "Ministry" refers to the officers of the church, especially those who preach the gospel. "Oracles" means the Scriptures, which are committed to the church as the source of her message and the guide for her life. "Ordinances" are the God-ordained functions of the church: worship, instruction, the sacraments, discipline. Christ continues to work in the church to make these things effective to accomplish His purpose. When He gave the Great Commission, Christ promised, "I am with you always, to the very end of the age" (Matt. 28:20).

## The Visibility and Purity of the Church

Sections 4 and 5 speak of degrees of visibility and purity in the visible church. Since the visible church is imperfect, particular parts of it are closer to, or further from, what Christ wants the church to be. The members of the Westminster Assembly were called "Puritans" because they were striving to bring the Church of England into closer conformity to the teaching of Scripture, to make it more pure.

The Assembly did not anticipate the division of the church into the multiplicity of denominations that exist today. In the light of churches being more or less pure, Christians face difficult choices regarding which branch of the church they should be part of. Church affiliation should not be a matter of heritage alone, or of personal likes and dislikes. We should seek to be obedient to Christ and to serve Him in a church where we may follow His Word with a good conscience. The *Confession* points to the sad reality of churches becoming apostate; when that happens, believers must separate from them.

Particular churches may lose the gospel, but Christ has promised to build His church (Matt. 16:18). We can be encouraged by the knowledge that the church will endure.

## Christ's Headship over the Church

The final section of the chapter deals with the precious doctrine of the sole headship of Christ over His church. This doctrine is taught clearly in Ephesians 1:20-22; 5:22-24; and Colossians 2:16-23. In Britain, the Covenanters and Puritans faced great suffering as they bore witness to this truth over against the pretensions of the Tudor and Stuart kings. Then and now, the Pope of Rome also claims to be head on earth of Christ's church. It is important still to maintain that we have only one Lord, Jesus Christ, "Zion's only King and Head."

# 26

## Real Happiness in Real Life

In his introduction to the *Reformed Confessions of the 16ᵗʰ Century*, Arthur Cochrane wrote, "It is too little known in Presbyterian Churches in the Anglo-Saxon world that the Westminster standards do not belong to the Reformation but are products of Puritanism and post-Reformation scholasticism. They reflect a legalism, moralism, and rationalism that are foreign to the confessions of a century earlier. They lack the spontaneity, freshness, and joyfulness of the Reformation" (p. 30).

Such a hostile assessment of the *Westminster Confession* and *Catechisms* is shocking in one who taught in a Presbyterian seminary professedly committed to those standards. More than that, his view is blatantly wrong, as a careful reading of the Westminster documents will show. The chapter now under consideration is enough to show how mistaken Prof. Cochrane's view is.

Parallels to chapter 25, "Of the Church," may be found in most of the earlier Reformed Confessions, but this chapter on "the Communion of Saints" has no adequate counterpart in other Confessions. Into its exposition of "union and communion" with Christ and other believers, it emphasizes the experiential and practical aspects of the life of the believer within the fellowship of the church.

Chapter 26 should be studied along with Questions 65–86 of the *Westminster Larger Catechism*, where the doctrine of our salvation is unfolded in terms of "union and communion with [Christ] in grace and glory."

## Union with Christ

First, the doctrine of union with Christ is expressed. "All saints [i.e., believers] that are united to Christ by his Spirit, and by faith, have fellowship with him in his graces, sufferings, death, resurrection, and glory." John Murray said that in our understanding of the Christian life, "nothing is more central or basic than union and communion with Christ" (*Redemption Accomplished and Applied*, p. 161). He points to the frequency with which the New Testament speaks about our being "in Christ," and Christ's being in us. By the work of the Holy Spirit in effectual calling, and by our believing response, we enter into a vital and spiritual union with Christ, in which the fullness of His grace and power come to be ours. We share now in the benefits of His suffering, death, and resurrection, and we will share His glory in the age to come.

The *Confession* speaks of our sharing in Christ's "graces." This should be understood as the gifts of grace that come from Him. The *Larger Catechism* speaks of effectual calling, justification, adoption, and sanctification as results of God's grace in Christ (Q. 67, 70, 74, 75) and calls faith and repentance "saving graces" (Q. 72, 76). Because they shared in these graces, believers experience, even in this life, the firstfruits of glory: "the sense of God's love, peace of conscience, joy in the Holy Ghost, and hope of glory" (Q. 83). Let the reader judge whether such teaching is legalistic, rationalistic, or lacking in joy!

Sharing in Christ's graces probably also means that by sanctification we are more and more conformed to the image of Christ, possessing the character qualities we see in Him (2 Cor. 3:18). United to Christ, believers are therefore united to each other. The reference to Christ as "their head" implies that the church, with its multiplicity and diversity of members, is His body, though that term is not used here. (The Scripture texts cited make it clear that this is what the *Confession* means.) Being part of the body of Christ carries both benefits and obligations. As such, believers share in each other's gifts and graces. The Spirit bestows on each Christian particular gifts, which are to be used for the benefit of the whole body (1 Cor. 12:7). As the graces of Christ appear in His people—love, joy, peace, patience, etc.—the fellowship of the church is a place of great blessing.

Our union with one another also carries responsibilities. Publicly and privately, we are to seek the good of fellow believers in all the ways available to us. This leads us to pay heed to the many "one another" passages in Scripture, which tell us how we are to make our love for one another practical in the church.

## Showing Love in the Church

Several ways that we are to do this are given in section 2 of the chapter. Our mutual participation in the worship of God is strengthening to others. In a day of great individualism, the gathering of God's people for worship needs to be strongly encouraged. When we assemble for worship, we not only glorify God, but we also strengthen and comfort one another (Heb. 10:19-25). The *Confession* mentions "other spiritual services." These include studying the Word together, praying with and for one another, and talking together about the things of the Lord.

Our ministry to one another is not to be limited to the "spiritual" things, but is to include what the *Confession* calls "outward things." Acts 2:42-46 gives us an example of how the body life of the Church is to function. In the *Form of Presbyterial Church-Government*, the Assembly followed Calvin and Knox in describing the office of deacon as a distinct and perpetual office in the church, with the particular responsibility for "distributing to the necessities of the poor." The matter of ministering in "outward things" is so important that Christ has instituted an office in the Church to give leadership in this task. Further, the *Form of Church-Government* provided that particular congregations should be made up of those who lived near to one another for the following reason: "The pastor and people must so nearly cohabit together, as that they may mutually perform their duties each to other with most conveniency." Reformed churches should give careful attention to the ministry of mercy, and to practical arrangements for carrying it out in the life of the congregation.

This section makes it clear that our concern is not to be limited to those of our own group, however. This mutual helpfulness "is to be extended unto all those who in every place call upon the name of the Lord Jesus." All those who are truly united to Christ are our brothers and sisters, whatever their denomination or nationality. The collection for the relief of famine sufferers in Jerusalem occupied Paul's attention and organizing skills for several years during his third missionary journey. Since the apostle, with his great zeal for evangelism, gave his time and energy to an international and intercultural ministry of mercy, the church today ought to follow his example.

## False Views of Union and Communion

The final section of the chapter warns against two false views regarding union and communion. The first was theological—the view that union with Christ removed the ultimate distinction between the Creator and the creature. Such pantheistic views, resembling New Age thought, were being circulated in Britain in the 17th century. The *Confession* responds, "This communion which the saints have with Christ doth not make them, in any wise, partakers of the substance of his Godhead, or to be equal with Christ, in any respect."

The second error was being taught by certain sectarian groups such as the "Family of Love." They held that Christians should give up all ownership of private property and become a communal society. The Assembly, however, did not regard the events described in Acts 2:44-46 as normative for the church in all situations. The right of private property is implied in the eighth commandment, and in Acts 5:4 Peter recognized the right of Ananias and Sapphira to keep what was their own. Therefore the *Confession* teaches that the communion of believers with one another does not "take away or infringe the title or property which each man hath in his goods and possessions."

The inclusion of this chapter on the communion of saints refutes the notion that the *Confession of Faith* is a scholastic, legalistic, moralistic, rationalistic document lacking spontaneity, freshness, and joyfulness. The chapter describes a relation with Christ that is deeply personal, intimate, and rich in blessing. It describes the church as a loving fellowship of people who love the Savior, and therefore love and care for one another. Such a church has been, and will be, a shining light in this dark world of sin, selfishness, and alienation.

# 27

# The Sacraments

The *Westminster Confession* devotes three chapters to the
sacraments. This reflects not only their basic importance
but also the fact that they were the subject of much disagreement in the Reformation period. Catholics, Lutherans,
Zwinglians, Anabaptists, and Calvinists differed from one
another on many points of baptism and the Lord's supper.
The most important differences were between the Catholic
Church and most Protestants. Those differences form the
immediate background of chapter 27.

If the reader has access to Calvin's *Institutes*, it will be
helpful to read his chapter on the sacraments (Book 4, Chap.
15). The *Confession* follows Calvin closely here, both in the
order of topics, and in the doctrinal positions taken.

## A Definition of Sacraments

The first section gives a definition of sacraments, and states
the functions they have in the church. The word *sacraments*
is not found in Scripture. It is from a Latin word used in the
Vulgate version to translate the Greek word *mystery*. In the early

church, "sacrament" was used in the sense of "signs which reverently represented sublime and spiritual things" (Calvin).

Sacraments are "signs and seals of the covenant of grace." As signs, they present to our senses the central truths of the gospel, "to represent Christ and His benefits." As seals, they "confirm our interest in Him." ("Interest" is used here in the sense of "having a claim on, or a share in.") Calvin uses the analogy of a seal on a government document, which confirms what is written and gives readers confidence in it.

Legitimate sacraments are not invented by human authority, but are "immediately instituted by God." In the controversy with the Catholic Church over the number of sacraments, the Reformers insisted that only two were authorized by God's Word for the New Testament church. The point is made in section 4 of this chapter.

In addition to portraying Christ and confirming our possession of Him and His benefits, two other functions of sacraments are mentioned. The sacraments "put a visible difference" between the church and the world, and "engage them [members of the church] to the service of God in Christ." These two functions are related to another way the word "sacrament" was used in Rome: It meant a soldier's oath of loyalty, and this is a secondary sense in which it is used of baptism and the Lord's supper, understanding them as pledges of our loyalty to Christ.

The sacraments, then, must be seen from a covenantal perspective. As they point to the gospel, they confirm God's promise, "I will be your God." As they express our commitment to Christ, they indicate our response to God's grace: "We are your people" (Rev. 21:3).

## Taking Sacraments Literally

One of the Reformation debates was about how literally one should interpret biblical language about the sacraments. Section 2 deals with this issue. Does baptism itself really wash away sins (Acts 22:16)? In the Lord's Supper, does one consume the actual flesh and blood of Christ (Luke 22:19-20)?

Catholics took such statements quite literally. The result was a belief that grace and salvation come through the channel of the sacraments, and that outside the Catholic Church no one could be saved.

The response of the Reformers was that such language was figurative. There is a close connection between the sign and what it points to. In a kind of shorthand, the Bible sometimes speaks of the sign as accomplishing salvation, when the real meaning is that it is Christ who gives salvation, using the sacrament as a means of instructing and strengthening our faith.

## The Efficacy of the Sacraments

Section 3 is stated in largely negative terms, but it makes a very positive point: The sacraments are effective; they are means of grace. By them, grace is "exhibited" and "conferred." These two words have the same meaning in this connection, with "exhibited" being used in its older sense of "granting" and "providing." This grace is given to "worthy receivers" when the sacraments are "rightly used."

As will be made clear in chapter 29, this requires faith on the part of the recipient. The Holy Spirit works in the life of the believer, enabling him or her to respond to the promises of the gospel. This is one of many places in the *Confession* where Word and Spirit are seen together. The Spirit works by and with the Word in our hearts to bring the benefits of Christ's saving work to us.

The negative statements of this section reject the Roman Catholic teaching on this subject. Rome taught that the sacraments are effective *ex opere operato*, that is, "on the basis of the action performed." This meant that the sacraments had the power to convey grace so long as the recipient did not place any barrier in the way. Active faith was not needed. The *Confession* rejects the view that the sacraments possess some inherent power to bless.

A second Catholic teaching was that, in order for a sacrament to be effective, the priest must have the intention to follow the teaching of the church about the sacraments. This was rejected by the *Confession* because it would make the efficacy of the sacraments depend on fallible men, whose real intention could never be known with certainty.

On the efficacy of the sacraments, Calvin cites Augustine regarding two errors to be avoided: "The first vice is for us to receive the signs as though they had been given in vain...to cause them to be wholly fruitless in us. The second vice is by not lifting our minds beyond the visible sign, to transfer to it the credit for those benefits which are conferred upon us by Christ alone. And they are conferred through the Holy Spirit, who makes us partakers in Christ" (*Institutes* IV.XIV.16).

## The Administration of the Sacraments

In addition to limiting the number of sacraments to two—baptism and the Lord's supper—section 4 restricts the administering of the sacraments. Only those who have been ordained as ministers of the gospel may administer them. One reason for this restriction is that the Catholic Church taught that in emergencies anyone could administer baptism, since it was necessary for salvation. Since the grace of Christ can come without baptism, lay baptism was rejected.

Another reason for the restriction is a matter of order. A. A. Hodge comments, "This is not said in the interest in any priestly theory of the ministry...But since the Church is an organized society, under laws executed by regularly appointed officers, it is evident that ordinances—which are badges of Church members,...the instruments of discipline, and seals of the covenant formed by the great Head of the Church with his living members—can properly be administered only by the highest legal officers of the Church, those who are commissioned as ambassadors for Christ to treat in his name with men" (p. 335).

## One Covenant of Grace

The final section of the chapter expresses again the view that there is one covenant of grace in all periods of history.

This covenantal theology leads to the statement, "The sacraments of the Old Testament…were, for substance, the same with those of the New." Circumcision and Passover in the Old Testament system pointed to Christ, as do baptism and the Lord's supper in the New.

Our discussion of this chapter may fitly be concluded with the words of Calvin: "I say that Christ is the matter, or (if you prefer) the substance of all the sacraments; for…they do not promise anything apart from Him…Therefore, the sacraments have effectiveness among us in proportion as we are helped by their ministry sometimes to foster, confirm, and increase the true knowledge of Christ in ourselves; at other times to possess him more fully and enjoy his riches. But that happens when we receive in true faith what is offered there" (*Institutes* IV.XIV.16).

# 28

# Baptism as a Sign of Grace

A s John Calvin had done in the *Institutes*, the *Confession* first discusses the teaching of Scripture about the sacraments in general. Then it gives special attention to the two sacraments of the New Testament, baptism and the Lord's supper. This arrangement is followed because there are also Old Testament sacraments, which are only mentioned in passing in chapter 27 (section 5).

## Baptism is a Sacrament

The first section of the present chapter identifies baptism as meeting the definition of a sacrament (see chap. 26, section 1). It was ordained by Christ. It is a sign and seal of the covenant of grace. By publicly admitting the one who receives it to the visible church, baptism marks the difference between the church and the world. By pointing to surrender of one life to God to walk in newness of life, it is a solemn engagement of the person to live a life of service to God.

As a sign, baptism represents Christ and His benefits. John Murray, in his book *Christian Baptism*, follows Calvin in seeing a threefold significance in this ceremonial washing. It portrays our union with Christ, our renewal by the Holy Spirit, and our cleansing from sin. These three things are expressed here in different words: "ingrafting into Christ," "regeneration," and "remission of sins." As usual, the proof texts should be consulted to see the biblical basis for this interpretation of the meaning of baptism.

As a seal, baptism confirms our interest in Christ. Calvin says that a sacrament is like the official seal on a government document, which gives authenticity to the message found there. Baptism is for the sake of our assurance; it confirms the promises of the gospel.

In Matthew 28:18-20, after Jesus had commanded His apostles to baptize those who became disciples, He added the promise, "And surely I am with you always, to the very end of the age." The promise and the command are for the same time period. For this reason, baptism is to continue until Christ returns.

## How Baptism is to be Performed

The second and third sections tell how baptism is to be performed. Since it is a ceremonial washing (*Westminster Shorter Catechism*, Q. 94), it requires the use of water. In explaining baptism, it is often said that the water signifies the blood of Christ, or the Holy Spirit, or both. However, the Scripture does not directly state this, and neither does the *Confession*. It seems best to avoid the confusion of saying that the water represents two different things (blood and Spirit), and to focus on the action of washing, which points to forgiveness and renewal through union with Christ.

Baptism is performed "in the name of the Father, and of the Son, and of the Holy Ghost." These words embody the doctrine of the Trinity, for there is one divine name, which designates three distinct persons. Rowland Ward writes, "Baptism speaks of a new relationship being cemented with the one into whose name you are baptized." The covenant of grace involves a relationship between the living God and redeemed sinners, which is confirmed by the ordinance of baptism.

Since baptism is fundamentally a ceremonial washing, the amount of water and the way in which it is applied are, according to the *Confession*, relatively unimportant. The *Confession* favors pouring or sprinkling but does not reject immersion as a valid mode of baptism. This view is favored by the covenantal language of Ezekiel 36:25-27, an important passage for understanding the symbolism: "I will sprinkle clean water on you, and you will be clean....I will give you a new heart and put a new spirit in you; I will remove from you your heart of stone and give you a heart of flesh. And I will put my Spirit in you and move you to follow my decrees and be careful to keep my laws....You will be my people, and I will be your God."

## Who is to be Baptized

The fourth section speaks of those who are to be baptized. For adults, it is "those that do actually profess faith in and obedience unto Christ." In a missionary situation, like that of the New Testament church, those who hear and respond to the gospel are baptized upon profession of faith, the kind of faith that leads to a commitment to obey Christ. In our increasingly secularized culture, we should expect that we will see many coming to receive adult baptism, as God blesses the preaching of the gospel.

However, baptism is not only for believing adults, but for their children. This has been a point of disagreement among Christians since the time of the Reformation. The case for infant baptism does not rest on a few proof texts, but on an understanding that God deals with His people by way of covenant. Since the Fall, God has been saving those whom He has chosen by the same covenant of grace. He revealed that covenant to Abraham, and gave him circumcision as its sign and seal (Gen. 17:3-14; Rom. 4:1-12). The fundamental meaning of circumcision was spiritual; it was not a sign of outward ceremonial holiness, but of the cleansing of the heart.

With the coming of Christ, the covenant sign was changed from circumcision to baptism (Col. 2:11-12). There was no indication, however, that the children of believers were now excluded from the covenant sign. Instead, a high proportion of the baptisms recorded in the New Testament were of households, pointing to the fact that God continued to deal with families, not just individuals, in His covenant. (For a fuller treatment of this subject, see Calvin's *Institutes*, Book IV, Chapter XVI, or John Murray's *Christian Baptism*.)

## Baptism Does Not Save

Section 5 of this chapter is responding to Roman Catholic teaching about baptism, which is found to some degree in Lutheran and Anglican doctrine. Since God has commanded the church to practice baptism, it is sinful to despise or neglect it. On the other hand, baptism does not in itself produce the new birth or salvation. Therefore, a person like the repentant thief on the cross, who had no opportunity to be baptized, was assured by Jesus that he would be in heaven (Luke 23:40-43). On the other hand, not everyone who receives baptism, whether adult or child, is born again. Baptism is only effective for those to whom God also grants the gift of true saving faith.

## The Effectiveness of Baptism

The efficacy (effectiveness) of baptism is the subject of section 6: "By the right use of this ordinance, the grace promised is not only offered, but really exhibited and conferred by the Holy Ghost, to such…as that grace belongeth to." (In this context, "exhibited" and "conferred" are synonyms.) The sacraments, including baptism, are means of grace. To understand this, however, we must remember the function of sacraments. They are for the confirmation and strengthening of faith in the Word. They do not operate in and of themselves, separately from the Word of God. Salvation comes from hearing and responding to the gospel. When a person has believed, then baptism has an impact in his or her experience, to give assurance of God's grace.

This function of baptism is not restricted to the time when it is actually administered. For an adult believer, the experience of being baptized is remembered, and that memory serves to strengthen faith. One who has been baptized as an infant comes to know and understand that fact and its meaning through the reports of parents or others. Then the Lord uses the knowledge to draw the person to the Savior, or to confirm his relationship with Him. In either case, baptism operated through faith in the Savior and His Word.

## Baptized Only Once

Baptism signifies the work of the grace of God in our lives, which has a definite beginning. At a certain time, we are given new life by the effectual calling of the Spirit; we are justified once and for all by believing in Christ; we are united with Christ in a relationship that can never be broken. Since these things are true, the last section of the chapter teaches that baptism is to be administered only once.

It seems appropriate to conclude our discussion of baptism by quoting Question 167 of the *Larger Catechism*: "How is our baptism to be improved by us?" (i.e., "How may we benefit from our baptism?") "The…duty of improving our baptism, is to be performed…by serious and thankful consideration of the nature of it, and of the ends for which Christ instituted it, the privileges and benefits conferred and sealed thereby, and our solemn vow made therein; by being humbled for our sinful defilement;…by growing up to assurance of pardon of sin, and of all other blessing sealed to us in that sacrament; by drawing strength from the death and resurrection of Christ, into whom we are baptized, for the mortifying of sin, and quickening of grace; and by endeavouring to live by faith to have our conversation in holiness and righteousness, as those that have therein given up their names to Christ; and to walk in brotherly love, as being baptized by the same Spirit into one body."

# 29

# The Lord's Supper

The observance of the Lord's supper has always been an important part of Christian worship. The supper was instituted by Christ Himself, on the eve of His crucifixion, with the instruction that it is to be observed "until he comes." In this chapter, the *Confession* teaches us the purpose of this sacrament (section 1); the manner of its proper observance (section 3); and the blessings that come to believers through this means of grace (section 7).

The Protestant Reformation was a time of fierce disagreement about the Lord's supper. The Reformers rejected the Roman Catholic view of the supper, but, sadly, they were unable to agree among themselves about its meaning and effects. Luther, Zwingli, and Calvin each developed distinctive views, which were then embraced by their followers. The *Confession* reflects this background of controversy in that a number of sections of this chapter are primarily negative. Sections 2, 4, and 6 contain rejections of Catholic views, and sections 7 rejects a key Lutheran tenet.

## The Purposes of the Lord's Supper

The first section presents six purposes of the Lord's supper. It is, first, a means of remembering Christ's death. The bread represents Christ's body that was broken for us; the cup represents His blood, poured out on the cross for the remission of our sins.

Second, the supper contains God's covenant promise to His people, sealing to us the benefits of Christ's saving work (defined in the *Shorter Catechism*, Q. 32-38, as justification, adoption, sanctification, etc.). The Lord invites us to share a meal with Him as a pledge of His love to us in Christ.

A third purpose is "their spiritual nourishment and growth in him." To reflect on what Christ has done for us, to embrace the promises of God that are ratified in this symbolic meal, will bring about growth in grace.

These first three purposes point us to what God has done and is doing for our salvation. The last three purposes have to do with our response to God's grace.

Partaking of the Lord's Supper is an expression of our "further engagement" to live as Christ requires. In baptism, we were engaged to be the Lord's; in the supper that engagement is renewed and deepened. The *Confession* speaks of the "duties" we owe to Christ, but we should not think of these duties as the fulfillment of impersonal rules. Living in the way Christ requires is the way to deeper fellowship with Him.

Therefore, the fifth purpose of the supper is to be "a bond and pledge of [our] communion with Him." In the Covenant of Grace, God promises to be our God, and we respond by promising to be His people. We make this bond and pledge as we come to the Lord's table. We come with the desire to have deeper fellowship with Christ as we live in obedience to Him (see John 14:21-23).

Finally, the Lord's supper is given to emphasize and deepen our fellowship with other believers. It is a "bond and pledge of [our] communion with each other, as members of His mystical body." This is why the supper is not to be administered privately (see section 4).

Calvin writes of the practical meaning of this: "We shall benefit very much from the Sacrament if this thought is…engraved upon our minds: that none of the brethren can be injured, despised, rejected, abused, or in any way offended by us, without at the same time, injuring, despising, and abusing Christ by the wrongs we do; that we cannot disagree with our brethren without at the same time disagreeing with Christ; that we cannot love Christ without loving him in the brethren; that we ought to take the same care of our brethren's bodies as we take of our own" (*Institutes*, IV.XVII.38). There is a clear connection between this communion and the "communion of saints."

## The Lord's Supper Is Not a Sacrifice

The second section rejects Catholic teaching about the purpose of the Lord's supper: It is not a sacrifice for the remission of sins. This teaching had been strongly asserted in the twenty-second session of the Council of Trent: "If anyone says that in the mass a true and real sacrifice is not offered to God…let him be anathema." The *Confession*'s answer is that the Scripture clearly teaches that Christ died "once for all" (Heb. 10:11-18).

## How to Observe the Lord's Supper

Section 3 outlines the simple way in which the Lord's supper is to be observed. There are no elaborate ceremonies prescribed. The minister, authorized by Christ, first proclaims the Word of God about the meaning of the supper in the "word of institution."

Since the benefit of the supper comes to those who have true, saving faith, it is essential that the sacrament is not separated from the Word. The minister prays, blessing the elements, which is explained as setting them apart from a common to a holy use. He takes and breaks the bread, and gives it to the communicants. He takes the cup and also gives it to the communicants. Thus are set before the congregation the historical facts of the gospel, the offer of Christ to them for their salvation, and their need to receive Him by faith.

## No Solitary Observance; No Worship of the Elements

Catholic practices related to the sacrament are rejected in the fourth section. There is to be no solitary observance. (The Lord's supper could be administered in private homes, but only if a congregation of at least two or three was present, and if there was some teaching from Scripture.) The laity were to receive the cup as well as the bread. Since Catholics believed that the elements truly became the actual body and blood of Christ, the elements were placed in special containers, and carried about in processions. The people were required to bow down and worship them as Christ, physically present. The Reformers rightly labeled this idolatry.

## Figurative Language about the Elements

Section 5 explains the language about the Lord's supper. Catholics and Lutherans took the words of Jesus about the supper very literally: "This is my body...this is my blood" (Matt. 26:26, 28; John 6:53-55). The position of the *Confession* is that such language is figurative, meaning, "This represents my body...my blood." Jesus often used such language: "I am the vine"; "I am the water of life"; "I am the light of the world." No one insists that these statements be taken in a literal way.

## Transubstantiation Is Wrong

The sixth section addresses and rejects the Catholic doctrine of transubstantiation. The Council of Trent asserted that in the mass a double miracle took place. When the priest uttered the words of consecration, the substance or essence of the elements was changed to the actual flesh and blood of Christ. By a second miracle these elements continued to have the qualities of bread and wine, in texture, smell, taste, etc. The *Confession* rejects this doctrine as being unbiblical and unreasonable.

## Christ is Active in the Lord's Supper

The Lutheran view of the presence of Christ in the Lord's supper is rejected in section 7: that the body and blood of

Christ are "in, with, and under" the bread and wine. Luther agreed that the substance or elements do not change, but he held that the actual body and blood are present, and are consumed by the communicants, whether believers or not. By contrast, the *Confession* teaches that Christ is "really, but spiritually, present to the faith of believers in that ordinance." The Lord's supper is not an empty ceremony. Christ is active in it by His Spirit, so that believers are truly blessed and built up in their relationship with Him.

Since saving faith is essential for benefiting from the Lord's supper, section 7 warns that those who are not believers should not partake. This is in keeping with Paul's warning in 1 Corinthians 11:28-32. But the decision of whether to participate is not left to the individual alone. The *Confession* says that "ignorant and ungodly persons" are not to "be admitted" to the Lord's table. This speaks of the necessity of church discipline, which is the subject of the next chapter of the *Confession*.

The warning about "unworthy coming" that is given here has troubled many people of sensitive consciences. It is good to consider the teaching of the *Larger Catechism* in Question 172: "One who doubteth of his being in Christ, or of his due preparation...may have a true interest in Christ, though he be not yet assured thereof; and in God's account of it hath it, if he...unfeignedly desires to be found in Christ, and to depart from iniquity: In which case (because promises are made, and this sacrament is appointed, for the relief even of weak and doubting Christians)...he may and ought to come to the Lord's supper, that he may be further strengthened."

# 30

# Church Censures

The *Westminster Confession* may be roughly divided into three sections. The first eight chapters deal with God and with His objective works of creation, providence, and redemption. Chapters 9–19 contain a rich description of how God applies the redemption purchased by Christ subjectively to the believer. Chapters 20–31 are mainly occupied with the doctrine of the Church. (Chapter 23, "Of the Civil Magistrate," is an exception, but even that chapter discusses the relation of the magistrate to the Church.) The two final chapters deal with eschatology, the doctrine of the "last things."

The present chapter, then, is part of the *Confession's* teaching on the Church and treats the important subject of church discipline. It needs to be interpreted in the light of two other documents of the Assembly, *The Form of Presbyterian Church Government* (FCG), and *The Directory for Church Government* (DCG). (The latter document, which is the Assembly's final and practical deliverance on the subject of church government, is little known, because it did not receive official approval in England or Scotland. A copy is found in *Pressing Toward the Mark*, ed. by Charles Dennison and Richard Gamble, pp. 83-98, published by the Orthodox Presbyterian Church.)

## Christ Appointed Church Government

The first section of chapter 30 makes the point that Christ has appointed a government in His Church, and that, according to that appointment, the responsibility for church discipline is committed to "church officers." Here the *Confession* articulates the regulative principle for church government, the conviction that the organization of the Church is not left to human wisdom, but that Christ has given directions for the permanent form of church government in His Word. The preface to the FCG quotes from Isaiah 9:6, Matthew 28:18, and Ephesians 1:19-23 and 4:7-11 to make this point. Reformed Presbyterians traditionally pray for the Lord's blessing upon official church actions "in the name of the Lord Jesus Christ, Zion's only King and Head," remembering the Covenanters' long struggle to defend Christ's authority in the church against usurpation by civil rulers.

## The Keys of the Kingdom

In the second section, the *Confession* gives the Reformed view of the meaning of the keys of the kingdom, which were spoken of by Jesus in Matthew 16:19. The Roman Catholic Church interpreted Jesus' words as a grant of supreme authority to Peter and to his successors in the papacy, an authority to grant or withhold salvation. The Reformed churches held that there was no provision in the New Testament for successors to the apostles, but that the "power of the keys" was exercised by the original apostles when they inscribed their witness in the New Testament, and thereby gave instructions for the qualifications and duties of church officers.

Those officers, called teaching and ruling elders, have a limited declarative and ministerial power. They use the power of the keys by preaching and teaching the Word of God, and by admitting persons to the fellowship of the church, or, if necessary, excluding others from the fellowship. Since only God knows the heart, and only God can forgive sins (1 Sam. 16:7; Mark 2:5-12), the declarations of ministers and elders are not the final word.

What the Assembly meant can be seen in "The Directory for Church Censures," which is part of the *DCG*. The formula for excommunication included these words: "I pronounce and declare thee excommunicated, and shut out from the communion of the faithful." Later, when such a person was brought to repentance, there was a statement for absolution: "I pronounce and declare thee absolved from the sentence of excommunication...and do receive thee to the ordinances of Christ, that thou mayest be partaker of all his benefits, to thy eternal salvation." This pronouncement was accompanied by prayer "for assurance of mercy and forgiveness to this penitent."

The minister made no direct statement about the damnation or salvation of the sinner. The power of the keys had to do with the relation of the person to the visible church. His ultimate spiritual state was left with God, the searcher of hearts.

## The Purposes of Church Discipline

The third section of the chapter deals with the multiple purposes of church discipline. It is, first, for the restoration of the offender, that he or she may be brought to repentance. Second, it is for the good of other church members, that they may be deterred from sinning. If the infection of sin were to spread, the whole church might fall under God's fatherly displeasure and chastening.

Finally, faithful church discipline is for the honor of Christ and the gospel. Christians bear the name of their Savior, and their disobedience reflects unfavorably upon Him. When the church tolerates open and obstinate sin, its witness to the saving power of the gospel is gravely compromised.

The *Confession* does not spell out in detail the kind of

offenses for which church discipline should be applied. This section does speak of "notorious and obstinate offenders," indicating that church discipline is especially needed when sins are public, and when private and personal admonition brings no response.

The *DCG* gives a more detailed treatment of this subject that follows quite closely chapter 20, section 4, of the *Confession*. According to the *DCG*, church discipline is for three kinds of offenses: errors that "subvert the faith...or overthrow the power of godliness"; "practices which cause the name of God to be blasphemed, and cannot stand with the power of godliness"; and practices that "subvert that order, unity and peace, which Christ hath established in his church."

The *DCG* allowed for some disagreement on points of doctrine, and for "sins of infirmity" in Christians, which do not call for public discipline. It also allowed for conscientious dissent from some outward regulations of worship and church government.

Most of the members of the Westminster Assembly had suffered at the hands of the bishops for their consciences, so they were inclined to be charitable to others who had problems of conscience. Church discipline was not to be a weapon with which to enforce outward conformity in matters that were not essential to the Christian faith.

## Three Steps of Church Discipline

The final section describes three steps of church discipline. First comes admonition, then temporary exclusion from participation in the Lord's supper, and finally, excommunication. Even excommunication was not necessarily permanent, for, when a sinner repented, he or she was readmitted to the church. Unlike suspension, however, excommunication was not for a stated time.

The *DCG* gives interesting information about the kind of admonition that should be given: "As there shall be cause, several public admonitions shall be given to the offender (if he appears) and prayers made for him....In the admonitions, let the fact be charged upon the offender, with the clear evidence of his guilt thereof; then let the nature of his sin, the particular aggravations of it, the punishments and curses threatened against it, the danger of impenitency, especially after such means used, the woeful condition of them cast out from the favor of God and communion of the saints, the great mercy of God in Christ to the penitent, how ready and willing Christ is to forgive, and the church to accept him upon his serious repentance. Let these, or the like particulars, be urged upon him out of some suitable places of the holy scriptures."

When we read this chapter, and the elaboration of it found in the *DCG*, we may well be concerned that our churches today do not often carry out this kind of thorough, earnest church discipline. No doubt there were some circumstances in the 17th century that were different from ours. The Assembly contemplated an inclusive, established church, in which all members of the nation would normally be members of the national church and entitled to participate in its ordinances. That would mean that many in the visible church would be unconverted. (Samuel Rutherford said of the members of the Church of Scotland in that time period, that not one in forty was truly converted.) Hence there would be a need for frequent and severe discipline. In our churches today, when church membership is, in a sense, voluntary, there is hopefully a greater emphasis on the need for conversion for those who become members. So church discipline in the sense of exclusion from fellowship is not so frequently necessary.

Having said that, this chapter forces us to examine ourselves as to the seriousness of our concern for those who have fallen into sin and do not repent; our care for protecting others against temptation; our zeal for the honor of Christ and the gospel. We need to hear and respond to the warnings against a false tolerance that we read in 1 Corinthians 5 and in Christ's message to the church of Thyatira (Rev. 2:18-29).

# 31

# Rightly Dividing Church and State

The Westminster Assembly was called together to advise the English Parliament regarding the doctrine, government, and worship of the Church of England. The topic of church government received much attention in the Assembly. Two other documents had already been completed before the *Confession of Faith* was written: *The Form of Presbyterial Church-Government*, and *The Directory for Government*.

## Exceptions to the Confession

The *Confession* deals with matters of church government in chapters 30 and 31, but, because of the earlier documents, not in detail or fullness. Because of this, the Church of Scotland accepted the *Confession of Faith* with a qualification: "That the not mentioning in this *Confession* the several sorts of ecclesiastical officers and assemblies, shall be no prejudice to the truth of Christ in these matters, to be expressed fully in the Directory for Government."

The Church of Scotland had another problem related to the second section of this chapter, having to do with the power of the civil magistrate in the calling of synods. Whereas the meeting of synods without being called by the magistrate is treated by the *Confession* as extraordinary, the Church of Scotland asserted that ministers and elders are "free to assemble together synodically…at the ordinary times, upon delegation from the churches, by the intrinsical power received from Christ, as often as it is necessary for the good of the Church so to assemble" (in standard editions of the *Confession*, p. 15). The RP Church of Ireland makes the same qualification. The RPCNA simply says in its *Testimony*, "We reject paragraph 2 [of Chap. 31] of the *Confession of Faith*." Other American Presbyterians have modified the language of the *Confession* itself.

## The Confession is Not Infallible

Even those who heartily embrace the doctrines of the *Westminster Confession* are not bound to regard the *Confession* as infallible. The fourth section of this chapter asserts that "All synods and councils since the Apostles' times…may err, and many have erred. Therefore they are not to be made the rule of faith or practice; but to be used as a help in both." Almost all Presbyterians today believe that the *Confession* erred in giving too much authority to the civil government over the church and its ruling bodies.

This fourth section provides indirect testimony to the fact that the *Confession* teaches the inerrancy of Scripture. Synods or councils are not to be the rule of faith and practice, because they are subject to error. By contrast, the first chapter of the *Confession* asserts in the second section that the Scripture is "given by inspiration of God, to be the rule of faith and life." The clear implication is that the Scripture is without error.

Having noted some difficulties in this chapter, let us give attention to the positive teaching it contains regarding the role of governing assemblies in the church.

## Rejection of Congregationalism

First, note that the terms "synods or councils" are used here in a general sense. They refer to official meetings of ministers and elders. Other documents of the Assembly make it clear that meetings in a graduated series of courts are meant, with the lower courts being under the authority of the higher ones. In this matter, the *Confession* rejects the principle of the Independents, or Congregationalists, that all church authority resides in the local congregation, and that wider assemblies have only an advisory role. The Assembly looked to the meeting of the apostles and elders in Acts 15 as a justification for their position. (See also the arguments in the *Form of Presbyterial Church-Government*.)

## The Jurisdiction of Church Courts

The third section of the chapter describes the kind of things that come under the jurisdiction of church courts: deciding in doctrinal disputes and ethical questions ("cases of conscience"); giving direction for the conduct of public worship and church government; and adjudicating complaints about improper or unjust actions.

The decisions of church courts are both ministerial and authoritative. "Ministerial" means that the courts have a servant role. They serve Christ, and are under His authority. They are to make their decisions on the basis of the teaching and principles of the Word, and have no independent authority (see chapter 20). But within that limitation, their decisions carry authority. Their decisions "are to be received with reverence and submission; not only for their agreement with the Word, but also for the power whereby they are made, as being an ordinance of God appointed thereunto in his word."

The *Confession* thus stands against the view of church authority that prevailed in both the Roman and the Anglican churches, which taught that bishops were not limited to the Word of God in their power to bind the conscience, but could follow their own wisdom.

The Reformation principle of "Scripture alone" is here applied to the matter of church authority and church government. The *Confession*'s view stands against the individualism and false ideas of freedom that characterize much of modern evangelicalism. Real, though limited, authority is given by Christ to the courts of His church, and His people are bound to respect that authority. (For the scriptural foundation for this view, reflect on the proof texts that are listed in chapter 30, section 1).

## The Authority of the Church and the State

In section 5, the *Confession* addresses the separate spheres of authority given to the civil magistrate and to the church. Church assemblies are to "handle, or conclude, nothing, but that which is ecclesiastical: and are not to intermeddle with civil affairs." This is an important principle, but it is liable to misunderstanding. It has been used to assert that the church should not concern itself with social and political evils, such as slavery, racism, or abortion.

However, anyone who reads the Old Testament prophets knows that they spoke out clearly about the evils of their day. G.I. Williamson's comment (in *The Westminster Confession of Faith for Study Classes*) helps to give the proper balance: "The Reformed concept of 'sphere sovereignty'...recognizes that God is supreme in every realm or sphere of life...[T]he law of God is quite as relevant in the political realm as in any other. Moreover, it is the task of the Church to teach the whole counsel of God, even as it pertains to political affairs. But there is a world of difference between the teaching of principles of the Word of God to members of the church and interference in the affairs of the State. It is the task of Christians as citizens to effect that which is in accordance with the Gospel" (p. 326).

The life of William Wilberforce is a powerful example of how this can work. As a young man, he was a wicked and worldly member of the House of Commons. When he was converted to Christ, he thought he should leave the Parliament and become a minister of the gospel. However, John Newton, the converted slave-ship captain, advised him to remain in the Parliament and to use his influence there for Christ and for righteousness. Wilberforce labored for some

30 years to end Britain's involvement in the African slave trade, and eventually that goal was achieved.

Church courts are not to be political pressure groups. But by teaching the truths of Scripture, the church encourages followers of Christ to be salt and light in the world.   ⊕

# 32

# What Happens When People Die

It is appropriate that the *Confession of Faith* should conclude with two chapters about the "last things," the events and experiences that lie in the future for every person. In a time when the Christian world is filled with confident predictions about details of prophetic fulfillment, most of which will turn out to be untrue, it is refreshing to turn to the *Confession*. Its teaching is sober and restrained, not going beyond what the Bible clearly teaches, telling us only what is important for us to know.

## Understanding Death

The first section of chapter 32 summarizes what will occur 1) at the physical death of a person, 2) at the time of the resurrection, and 3) in the period in between, which theologians call "the intermediate state." Death involves a separation of the two constitutional parts of human nature, the body and the soul. Our bodies, in fulfillment of the pronouncement made to Adam after he sinned, return to the elements from which they were formed, "for dust you are, and to dust you will return" (Gen. 3:19). Our souls, the immaterial aspect of our being, do not undergo a similar disintegration, but rather "return to God." The *Confession* here uses almost verbatim the language of Ecclesiastes 12:7.

Recent Reformed theologians have emphasized the essential unity of body and soul in our being, rejecting the Greek view that the soul is inherently pure and immortal, and that our sin and imperfection is the consequence of being imprisoned in material bodies. The biblical view is that, when God had completed the work of creation, He looked upon all He had made, including the material aspects of it, and declared it to be "very good" (Gen. 1:31). Salvation is not accomplished by ridding us of that which is material, but by cleansing and transforming our whole being to make us like Christ. (See 1 Thess. 5:23.)

Some have charged that, in this section, the *Confession* adopts the Greek view of the essential immortality of the soul, since it says of souls that they "neither die nor sleep," but have an "immortal subsistence." The *Confession*, however, does not say that souls *cannot* die, but that they *will not* die or sleep. Furthermore, they have an immortal subsistence. The choice of the word "subsistence" appears to have been carefully made. In the 17th century, this term was commonly used to mean "continued existence, continuance" (see the *Oxford English Dictionary*). The *Confession* follows the teaching of the Bible that souls do exist eternally, without using the metaphysical ideas of the Greek philosophers that souls are indestructible. Souls exist eternally because God providentially maintains their existence.

Souls "return to God" to appear before Him in judgment (Heb. 9:27). That judgment results in a separation, even before the Last Great Judgment Day. Those who have been made righteous by justification, and in whom the work of sanctification has been progressing, have all traces of sin finally removed from them. This teaching of final sanctification is based on the fact that departed believers are called "just men made perfect" (Heb. 12:23), and also on the teaching that sinners are not allowed to appear in the presence of God (Ps. 15). The perfected saints behold the face of God; they enjoy His presence, acceptance, love, and fellowship. Though it is not cited as a proof text, the authors of the *Confession* probably had in mind Psalm 17:15: "And I—in righteousness I will see your face; when I awake, I will be satisfied with seeing your likeness." Such blessedness, though greatly to be desired, is not yet the complete fulfillment of our hope, for in the intermediate state we will await the resurrection, which will be the "full redemption" of our bodies.

## After Death for Unbelievers

Solemnly, the *Confession* also addresses what is in store for the wicked, those who have persisted in their rebellion against God and His Christ. They will be "cast into hell," described here as a place of darkness and suffering. They, too, anticipate a resurrection, but a resurrection of judgment.

In reaction to Roman Catholic teaching, the *Confession* teaches that "beside these two places for souls...the Scripture acknowledgeth none." This is primarily a rejection of the doctrine of purgatory. According to Catholic doctrine, purgatory is a place for souls in the intermediate state who died in grace but are in need of further cleansing from sins called "venial" (excusable), or who need to complete their own payment of the temporal punishment of sin.

The Protestant Reformation rejected the doctrine of purgatory on two grounds. First, it has no foundation in Scripture, as is stated here in the *Confession*. A recent Catholic instructional manual acknowledges this: "The word 'purgatory' is not in the Bible, nor is the doctrine of purgatory explicitly taught there" (*The Teaching of Christ*, Lawler, Wuerl, and Lawler, ed., p. 527). The Reformation principle of "Scripture alone" rules out the doctrine of purgatory as part of the official teaching of the Church. A second objection to the doctrine of purgatory is that it does not do justice to the nature of Christ's atonement as the complete sacrifice for sin: "because by one sacrifice he has made perfect forever those who are being made holy" (Heb. 10:14).

## The Resurrection of the Dead

The second section of chapter 32 speaks of the resurrection of the dead. This is called the "general resurrection," because it involves all human beings who have died, whether believers or not. The *Confession* here follows straightforwardly what is asserted in Daniel 12:2 and John 5:28-29. The time of this occurrence is "the last day," and the resurrection of the righteous and the wicked is simultaneous.

Skeptics reject the possibility of resuscitation of a corpse, but the Scripture teaches that God can do what seems impossible. The initial creation of all things out of nothing, after all, requires nothing less than the power of God. Since God can create life, He can also raise the dead.

There are limits to our ability to comprehend such a stupendous event in the light of our present experience and understanding. Our resurrection bodies will in some way be a continuation of our present bodies, but will also be different. That which is now characterized by corruptibility, dishonor, and weakness will in the resurrection be incorruptible, honorable, and powerful. This will be the wonderful work of our Savior.

There will be one group of people who will not experience death and resurrection—those who are still living at the time of Christ's return. Without undergoing the disintegration of death, they will be changed so as to share in the glory of resurrection life (1 Cor. 15:51; 1 Thess. 4:17).

## The Righteous and the Wicked

The third section of the chapter asserts the difference between the righteous and the wicked in the resurrection. All will have their bodies restored, but how different is the outcome! The resurrection of believers will be to honor, and conformity to Christ. The resurrection of unbelievers will be to dishonor, and to eternal separation from the favorable presence of God.

These words were written on the day following a horrendous terrorist attack. As we struggle to comprehend these things, we take refuge in the Lord of life and death.

None of us knows what a day may bring forth—hence the urgency of our efforts at evangelism. When we are in Christ, we can face a future which is, humanly speaking, filled with uncertainty. Yet we can be certain that our Savior will never leave us or forsake us. We can be certain that "if the earthly tent we live in is destroyed, we have a building from God, an eternal house in heaven, not built by human hands" (2 Cor. 5:1). We can be certain that the Savior whom we eagerly await from heaven, the Lord Jesus Christ, "by the power that enables him to bring everything under his control, will transform our lowly bodies so that they will be like his glorious body" (Phil. 3:20-21). Let us share the message of the gospel with others, so they can share with us these precious certainties.

# 33

# The Last Judgment

I t is fitting that the *Westminster Confession* should conclude with a presentation of what the Scriptures teach about the end of this age, the end of the world. In God's plan and providence, all of history moves toward this goal.

Teaching about the day of judgment fills the Scriptures. This chapter begins with a virtual quotation from Acts 17:31: "God hath appointed a day, wherein He will judge the world in righteousness, by Jesus Christ." There are about 50 references to that "day" in the New Testament, some 21 of them in the words of Jesus Himself. Much of the language of this chapter is drawn directly from Scripture, and presents in a clear and sober way, without speculation, what the Bible teaches on this subject.

## Who Will Be Involved in the Judgment

The first section identifies the persons who will be involved in the judgment. The judge will be none other than the exalted Lord Jesus Christ. It is the climactic act of His mediatorial kingship that He should judge the whole world;

this is part of the commission given to Him by His Father (John 5:22-23). Because, in the words of Psalm 45:6, the scepter of His kingdom is a scepter of righteousness, we can be confident that, in that awesome day, the judgment will be carried out in perfect righteousness. In this world where justice is often imperfect, it is a comfort to know that in the end evil will be punished and good will be rewarded (see Psalm 73).

Fallen, evil angels will appear before Christ in that day (Jude 1:6; 2 Pet. 2:4). On this mysterious subject the *Confession* limits itself to what the Bible actually says. Good angels are not mentioned. A. A. Hodge, citing Matthew 13:41-42 and 2 Thessalonians 1:7-8, says that they will be "attendants and ministers" in this grand tribunal (p. 391).

More directly relevant to us, all persons (i.e., humans) who have ever lived will appear. Each of us will give an account to God of how we have used his gift of life. The judgment is based on more than outward behavior. It will examine our words, which express what is truly in the heart (Matt. 12:33-37). Even our thoughts, often unknown to others, will be made known as we stand before Christ. On the basis of that searching judgment, then we are to receive in accord with what we have done while we lived.

## Dread and Despair?

Were we reading this chapter in isolation from others, we would at this point be filled with dread and despair. The *Westminster Shorter Catechism* teaches that we break the commandments daily, "in thought, word, and deed" (Q. 82). The only possible verdict in that great judgment, it seems, must be, "Guilty!"

But the *Confession* contains a "system of doctrine"; one chapter must not be viewed in isolation from others. Awareness of Christ's righteous judgment drives us back to the gospel, to a way in which sinners can become righteous before God. That way of salvation has been set forth especially in chapter 7, "Of God's Covenant with Man," in chapter 8, "Of

Christ the Mediator," and in chapter 11, "Of Justification."
In justice, we stand condemned. In His great mercy, God has
sent His own Son to fulfill the law on our behalf and to bear
the penalty we deserve.

A. A. Hodge writes, "The saints will not be acquitted in
the day of judgment on the ground of their own good deeds,
but because their names are found written in the...book of
God's electing love, and on the ground of their participation in the righteousness of Christ. Their good deeds will be
publicly cited as the evidences of their union with Christ"
(*Commentary*, p. 392).

## The Purpose and Outcome of the Judgment

Section 2 of the chapter covers two subjects: the aim or
purpose of the judgment, and its outcome.

The aim of the judgment is the glory of God, in the
demonstration of His mercy and of His justice, in order
that He may be praised. At the end of his long discussion
of the sovereignty of God in salvation and condemnation
in Romans, Paul concludes with a doxology, a heightened
expression of praise: "O the depth of the riches both of the
wisdom and knowledge of God! how unsearchable are his
judgments and his ways past finding out!...For of him, and
through him, and to him, are all things: to whom be glory
for ever. Amen" (Rom. 11:33, 36).

The outcome of the judgment is twofold. The righteous,
that is, those who have been made righteous by the saving
work of Christ, enter into eternal life and blessedness.

The wicked, described as "those who know not God and
obey not the Gospel of Jesus Christ" (see 2 Thess. 1:7-8), enter
into eternal punishment. In setting forth this solemn doctrine
of the eternal punishment of the wicked, the *Confession* is
content to repeat the clear expressions of Scripture, which
are given in the proof texts.

The destiny of unrepentant sinners is horrible to con-
template. There are professedly Christian teachers who deny
that there will be eternal punishment. William Barclay, for

example, states that he is "a convinced universalist," believing that everyone will ultimately be saved. Karl Barth denied that there is any life after death, either of blessing or punishment. Even John Stott and Philip Hughes, while teaching that there will be punishment for the wicked after death, expressed doubt that the punishment would be unending.

We can understand the sentiments that would lead to such views. However, our belief must be founded on the Word of God, and that Word teaches eternal punishment. We must bow before the Word, and remember that we are not more just or compassionate than God. He is the Judge of all the earth, who will surely do right (Gen. 18:25).

There is an interesting symmetry in the language of this section, in a double use of the expression "from the presence of the Lord." The saved will receive "that fullness of joy and blessing, which shall come from the presence of the Lord" (Acts 3:19). The wicked, on the other hand, will "be punished with everlasting destruction from the presence of the Lord" (2 Thess. 1:9). On that day, the presence of the Lord will be the source of fear, regret, and despair to those who have rejected Him. To those who have received and rested on Jesus Christ for salvation, the presence of the Lord will be the source of inexpressible comfort, thankfulness, and joy.

## Practical and Experiential Concern

We have repeatedly noticed in the course of these studies that the *Westminster Confession of Faith*, far from being a cold, sterile discussion of theology, is deeply concerned with the experiential aspects of the Christian faith. In the last section of this chapter, we find that practical and experiential concern expressed again. The section speaks of the certainty of the occurrence of the judgment day, and also of the uncertainty (from our perspective) of the time of its occurrence.

The Lord has clearly revealed the fact that there will be a day of judgment, to deter men from sin. The writers of the *Confession* had 2 Peter 3:11-14 in mind. In the light of the whole *Confession*, however, we should add the thought that it is not enough for people to try to avoid sinning in order to be ready for judgment. Beyond that, knowing that they have in fact sinned, and sinned greatly, people must flee to Christ in order to be clothed in His righteousness, and thus be ready for the judgment day.

For those who have trusted in Christ, contemplation of the Last Great Day is a source of great consolation. It will mean the end of the struggle with sin, the end of persecution, the end of suffering. Knowing that in the end our Lord Jesus will make all things right gives us patience to endure the present afflictions of life.

## No Man Knows the Day or the Hour

Finally, the time of the second coming of Christ and the day of judgment is unknown to us. This is the clear teaching of Jesus, for example, in the parable of the wise and foolish virgins (Matt. 25:1-13). Therefore we must always be watchful, always engaged in the worship and service to which our Lord has called us.

The *Confession* closes with the words that are found at the very end of the Bible, expressing our eagerness for the Lord to come, that we may be with Him forever: "Come, Lord Jesus, come quickly. Amen" (Rev. 22:20).

# Works Cited

Aquinas, Thomas. *Summa Contra Gentiles*. Book III. Notre Dame, Ind.: University of Notre Dame Press, 1976.

Barclay, William. *William Barclay: A Spiritual Autobiography*. Grand Rapids: Eerdman's, 1975.

Boettner, Loraine. *The Reformed Doctrine of Predestination*. Grand Rapids: Eerdman's, 1932.

---. *Studies in Theology*. Grand Rapids: Eerdman's, 1953.

*Book of Common Prayer*. 1549.

Bridges, Jerry. *Trusting God*. Colorado Springs: NavPress, 1988.

Calvin, John. *Institutes of the Christian Religion*. Philadelphia: The Westminster Press, 1960.

---. *Commentaries on Amos, Calvin's Commentaries*. Grand Rapids: Baker Book House, 1979.

---. Commentaries on 1 John, *Calvin's Commentaries*. Grand Rapids: Baker Book House, 1979.

---. Commentaries on Ephesians, *Calvin's Commentaries*. Grand Rapids: Baker Book House, 1979.

Cochrane, Arthur C. *Reformed Confessions of the 16th Century*. Philadelphia: The Westminster Press, 1966.

Denton, Michael. *Evolution: A Theory in Crisis*. Bethesda, Md.: Adler & Adler, 1986.

*Erasmus-Luther: Discourse on Free Will*. Ernst F. Winter, ed. New York: The Continuum Publishing Company, 1988.

"The Form of Presbyterial Church Government." *The Westminster Confession of Faith*. Glasgow: Free Presbyterian Publications, 2003.

Gillespie, George, *A Dispute Against the English Popish Ceremonies Obtruded on the Church of Scotland*. Dallas: Naphtali Press, 1993.

Hodge, A. A. *The Westminster Confession: A Commentary*. Edinburgh: Banner of Truth Trust, 2002.

*Irish RP Testimony*. Belfast: Graham and Heslik, 1966.

Johnson, Phillip E. *Darwin on Trial*. Downers Grove, Ill.: InterVarsity Press, 1993.

Kushner, Harold S. *When Bad Things Happen to Good People*. New York: Schocken Books, 1981.

Lee, Francis Nigel. *The Covenantal Sabbath*. London: The Lord's Day Observance Society, 1966.

Murray, John. *Christian Baptism*. Philadelphia: The Committee on Christian Education, The Orthodox Presbyterian Church, 1952.

---. *Collected Writings of John Murray*, vol. 2. Carlisle, Pa.: The Banner of Truth Trust, 1977.

---. *Redemption Accomplished and Applied*. Grand Rapids: Eerdman's, 1988.

*Oxford English Dictionary*. Second edition. New York: Oxford University Press, 1991.

Packer, J. I. *Knowing God*. Downers Grove, Ill.: InterVarsity Press, 1973.

*Pressing Toward the Mark*. Charles G. Dennison, Richard C. Gamble, eds. Philadelphia: The Committee for the Historian of the Orthodox Presbyterian Church, 1986.

Russell, Bertrand. *Mysticism and Logic*. New York: W. W. Norton, Inc., 1929.

Sande, Ken. *The Peacemaker*, Second edition. Grand Rapids: Eerdman's, 1953.

Schaff, Philip. "Second Helvetic Confession." *Creeds of Christendom*, vol. 3. Grand Rapids: Baker Book House, 1966.

---. "Thirty-Nine Articles of the Church of England." *Creeds of Christendom*, vol. 3. Grand Rapids: Baker Book House, 1966.

---. "The Irish Articles." *Creeds of Christendom*, vol. 3. Grand Rapids: Baker Book House, 1966.

Skinner, B.F. *Beyond Freedom and Dignity*. New York: Alfred A. Knopf, 1972.

*The Teaching of Christ: A Catholic Catechism for Adults*. Ronald Lawler, Donald W. Wuerl, Thomas Comerford Lawler, eds. Huntington, Ill.: Our Sunday Visitor, Inc.: 1975.

Ward, Rowland. *The Westminster Confession for the Church Today*. Melbourne: Presbyterian Church of Eastern Australia, 1992.

Warfield, Benjamin Breckinridge. *The Westminster Assembly and Its Work*. Cherry Hill, N.J.: Mack Publishing Company, 1972.

Whitaker, William. *A Disputation on Holy Scripture: Against the Papists especially Bellarmine and Stapleton*. Morgan, Pa.: Soli Deo Gloria Publications, 2000.

Williamson, G.I. *The Westminster Confession of Faith for Study Classes*. Second edition. Phillipsburg, N.J.: Presbyterian & Reformed, 2004.